Cityscapes

Cityscapes

Eight Views from the

Urban Classroom

Howard Banford
Myron Berkman
Carole Chin
Christine Cziko
Bob Fecho
Deborah Jumpp
Carole Miller
Marci Resnick

Berkeley, California
National Writing Project
1996

Please direct reprinting requests and book orders to:

National Writing Project
615 University Hall, #1040
University of California
Berkeley, CA   97420-1040

Telephone 510-642-0963
Fax 510-642-4545

Library of Congress Cataloging-in-Publication Data

Cityscapes: Eight views from the urban classroom / Howard Banford ... [et al.].
    p. cm.
    Includes bibliographical references.
    ISBN 1-883920-10-8
    1. English language — Composition and exercises — Study and teaching
(Elementary) — United States — Case studies. 2. English language-Composition
and exercises — Study and teaching (Secondary) — United States — Case studies. 3.
Creative writing (Elementary) — United States — Case studies. 4. Creative writing
(Secondary) — United States — Case studies. 5. Education, Urban — United States
— Case studies. 6. Multicultural education — United States — Case studies. I.
Banford, Howard, 1954 – . II. National Writing Project (U.S.)
LB1576.C557 1996
808'.042'071 — dc20

                                                                    95-47453
                                                                         CIP

Design and Layout: Paul Molinelli
Cover Design: William Peterson
All Photos: Elizabeth Crews
Editors: Art Peterson, Joe Check, Miriam Ylvisaker

Contents

Introduction

The Urban Sites Network of the National Writing Project: "Hard Talk" Among Urban Teachers

The Urban Sites Network of the National Writing Project was conceived, designed and implemented as a national teacher inquiry network for urban sites of the National Writing Project. Supported by a grant from the DeWitt Wallace-Reader's Digest Fund for three years, the goal of the Urban Sites Network has been to develop, articulate and implement a new agenda for National Writing Project sites serving large cities. It was developed within the NWP in response to the perception of many urban teachers that much of the research in education did not focus on the reality of schools in large cities. At the same time, there was a growing awareness among Writing Project teachers and directors that too few teachers of color were participating in Project activities. Writing Projects in major cities set out to diversify and strengthen leadership among teachers and Writing Project directors, to build the capacity of their own sites to deliver sustained, high quality professional development to teachers working in urban schools, and to bring to the attention of the National Writing Project and the educational community at large the critical issues and problems facing teachers and students in urban schools, as well as approaches and techniques for responding to them.

Over the three years of the project, a diverse group of 120 K-12 teachers developed and conducted structured, two-year inquiry studies of their classrooms or schools. Teachers at Urban Sites summer institutes raised difficult questions: How can we ensure that students in our classrooms are learning? How do we help students represent their thinking in writing? How can children's cultural backgrounds be used to support learning and how do we involve parents and communities in that effort? How do we demonstrate and assess children's progress? How do race and social class influence the way we understand and talk to each other and to our students? We set out to look closely at our classrooms in order to begin to answer some of these questions.

Over half of the teachers and coordinators who participated in Urban Sites Network activities are teachers of color. For many of us who came to USN summer institutes, this was the first time we had ever talked about race and ethnicity as they related to education in a setting where all groups under discussion were present. Discussions held during the summers came to be known as "hard talk" as we focused on what we must do to be both more effective and more compassionate teachers. We asked ourselves: What do I have to know to teach the children in my school and city? What beliefs do I have that may be standing in the way of my being a better teacher? What do I think, say or do that silences or opens the conversation among my colleagues, my students and their families?

The eight teacher inquiry studies which make up this book are a part of the effort to answer some of the difficult questions we raised. Through their studies, you will meet eight teachers who are not afraid of change, who are willing to challenge their own cherished beliefs, who are trying to see through the eyes of their students and their families. We are building, in the National Writing Project, a community of educators that can undertake, along with parents and others, the hard work that must be done to redress the vast inequalities plaguing education in our large urban centers.

Richard Sterling
Executive Director, National Writing Project

My Third Spaces: From Sharkey's to the Urban Sites Network

We were sitting around my dining room table, five urban student teachers and I, celebrating the imminent end of their program. Chris remarked he actually liked the humus, having eaten it once before when another old hippie served it to him. For a few minutes, the talk spun around, postponing the inevitable. Then, as it so often goes when teachers get together, the stories came tumbling out: "There's one student in my morning class…" "The other day I wanted to try something different, so…" "A strange thing happened on Tuesday, and I'm not sure how I should have handled it." For two hours we spoke of specifics and particularities which, in that wonderful story-way, became general and communal through the group's collective response. Finally the evening drew to a close with talk about graduation and being a first year teacher. They asked for my advice. So I told them to keep doing just what we had been doing with regularity throughout their student teaching: gathering with good professional friends, going public with their teaching, inviting thoughtful response, staying open and optimistic. And I also told them about Sharkey's Cove.

In 1979 I walked through the doors of Westminster Senior High School. I was prepared with a teaching credential but without a clue. During that crazy, exhilarating year, it was Sharkey's Cove where I found an anchor. A seafood tavern about a mile from school, Sharkey's was a comfortable cave strewn with fake buoys, fishing net curtains, and varnished wood rescued from old sail boats. Two hours from the Chesapeake Bay, Sharkey's always had plenty of 10-cent oysters and 90-cent draft. For those two reasons, it quickly became the permanent home of the bi-weekly meeting of the Westminster High School Faculty Pub Evaluation Committee. Every second Friday, paychecks in hand, an assortment of faculty came for the oysters and the beer, but most especially for the talk; and it was within the context of that talk about teaching, the stories and the response, that I learned to become a teacher. We met as a group for five years, dwindling away after Sharkey's itself was razed for a Jiffy Lube, and in its absence it was all the clearer what Sharkey's had done for us. It was not merely through our teaching, our time in the trenches, that we learned and grew as professionals; it was the teaching combined with the talk about the teaching. We needed real colleagues. We needed a public culture of teaching. Sharkey's had provided a core setting for an elusive type of collegial talk, talk which sadly did not occur in our faculty room or department offices.

I next found that wonderful teacher talk at the Maryland Writing Project. As I learned about other Writing Projects, as well as my own, I came to understand again and again that Writing Projects provide core settings for professional friendships and collegiality. They are places where we can make sense of our lives as teachers by making our teaching public and surrounding it with talk. The sociologist Ray Oldenburg would call the tavern Sharkey's Cove a "Third Place," a gathering place for public association beyond the separate realms of working life and domestic retreat. The more I see of Writing Projects, the more I believe they are a "third space," a place where teachers can create a public life.

As Writing Project teachers, our third spaces are convivial, filled with good teacher talk, but also demanding. Here we are asked to push beyond the easy or the self-serving story. We examine our teaching with depth and honesty. We share and question at the same time. Like my group at Sharkey's Cove, we are invited to stick with each other over time. There's time to think and then come back in two weeks to talk some more.

Back at my dining room table, Loralee expresses what each of my student teachers has learned: "Teaching is *hard,* harder than I ever dreamed, and city schools are *really hard.*" For my students, most of whom will become urban teachers, I have no greater wish than that they will find third spaces in their professional lives. If they find them, I trust that they will learn how to become teachers, and relearn and revise throughout their careers. But they note the absence of Sharkey's Coves in many teachers' lives. They say that many of their schools are not safe places, that teachers disperse to homes outside the communities where they teach, that the daily experience of stultifying school bureaucracies can have an deadening effect on the minds and the hearts of teachers and students alike. They've been coming together, they note, because they are students together in a teacher education program. Once they graduate, faced with the exhaustion of being a new teacher and the challenges of urban schools, will they organize a Sharkey's Cove for themselves?

It is because their complaints capture an important truth that urban Writing Projects are so important, a lesson I learned with my colleagues in Baltimore. Equally important are the positive examples of urban teachers who continue to learn and grow, to go public with their teaching, and to create with other teachers a third space. In *Cityscapes,* the National Writing Project has brought together the classroom research of eight teachers affiliated with the Urban Sites Network, a loose federation of urban Writing Projects supported by DeWitt Wallace-Reader's Digest Fund dedicated, in part, to creating long-term communities where urban teachers can ask questions about their classrooms and examine their practice. These teachers are operating in a third space: they are members of a professional community — a Writing Project inquiry group — that invites members to make their teaching public and to consider it over time. Their work as teacher colleagues is thoughtful, often meticulous, and deeply

collaborative. Stories result — expansive, specific, and particular — which, in that wonderful story-way, become general and
communal. The effect, for me, is not all that different from an
evening around my dining room table or a Friday afternoon at
Sharkey's Cove.

Elyse Eidman-Aadahl
Director, Maryland Writing Project

Looking at Students
One at a Time

Looking at Students One at a Time

During the past decade teachers have found new ways to examine and, consequently, to improve on teaching and learning in their classrooms. One of these breakthroughs has come with the understanding that often more can be gained by moving in for a close-up of one student rather than by pulling back for a long shot of an entire classroom of students. In the following case studies, Howard Banford and Myron Berkman follow single students through several months of learning experiences. In so doing they find out a great deal not only about Maricar and Marisol — the stars of these studies — but also about themselves as teachers. By looking closely at one student, these teachers find ways to better work with all their students.

The Blooming of Maricar:

Writing Workshop and the

Phantom Student

by

HOWARD BANFORD

EVERY teacher has a student like Maricar. She is the quiet girl, the one I could not remember when I sat down to make out the seating chart three weeks into the semester. She is, in the expression I learned from my Urban Sites colleague Marceline Torres, one of the "phantom students," one of those children whose voices are heard little or not at all in whole class discussions and daily classroom talk.

Maricar worked on individual class assignments in silence, surrounded by the soft roar of her more interactive classmates. She didn't participate in whole group discussions or volunteer to share her writing with the class. When students had the opportunity to choose a partner for an activity, she was usually not chosen, though she seemed pleasant and didn't offend other students. At recess she played by herself, dribbling a basketball and practicing her shooting skills. Maricar was a loner.

In short, Maricar operated on her own wave length and did not seem like the ideal candidate for a writing workshop, a form of classroom organization I have used for eight years in my Vallejo, California, second grade class, ever since being won over to the model presented in Donald Graves' *Writing: Teachers and Children at Work.* A well-functioning writing workshop demands cooperation and a certain gregariousness. In writing workshop, students not only choose their own topics and work at their own pace, but share stories in "author's chair" and respond to each other's work.

I know from previous experience that quiet students *do* make significant progress in a writing workshop setting, but I had never paid much attention to how this growth comes about. Before I undertook this study, if you had asked me about the writing workshop I would have said, "Everyone loves it." But in fact, the "everyone" here would be the six or seven most vocal students who would write things like:

> *I think writing work shop is fun because you get to write funny stuf and it is good practkis if one us wonts to be a artist or writer when we grow up because you get to draw pitchers and you write. Its like having a advenchure*
> *— Nick*

But I had not paid much attention to the specifics of how an isolated student like Maricar responds to writing workshop. I now wanted to see writing workshop through her eyes. I was interested in how writing workshop met her needs and the needs of others like her, and what a close look at Maricar could teach me about improving writing workshop and student learning in general.

For one school year from August to July, I observed Maricar and her involvement in the workshop. I carefully collected her writing from eighty-six writing workshop sessions, made audio tapes of her response group, interviewed her several times, and wrote regularly in my journal about what I saw. I've concluded that Maricar grew from the writing workshop in ways I would not have anticipated.

Maricar is Motivated by a Supportive Family

Maricar's family was certainly a factor in her growth. Although Maricar did not come to my class with stellar recommendations from her previous teachers, she did have the nurture of a loving home. Maricar's kindergarten teacher remembered her as a below average student, a slow worker, unsure of herself and very quiet. Her first grade teacher also told me that Maricar had worked very slowly and had difficulty with reading. She emphasized that Maricar had been a candidate for retention but had made some growth toward the end of the year because of the tremendous support she had received from her family.

Maricar, who was bilingual in English and Tagalog, lived with her Philippine born parents and five-year-old sister. Her father was in the Navy. Her mother worked as an accounting clerk. At home the family spoke primarily Tagalog, and Maricar's grandmother who took a great deal of responsibility for Maricar's after-school care, spoke to her grandchildren only in Tagalog. As with many immigrant families, Maricar's family strongly encouraged her education, and she had high expectations for herself.

I got a hint of Maricar's strong motivation when she responded to the first writing assignment before she became involved in writing workshop. I asked all students to write a letter explaining what they wanted to learn in second grade. Maricar wrote slowly, spending much time thinking and erasing. She worked for forty-five minutes on her letter, completing it during recess. Her letter read:

> *A Letter For Mr. Banford*
> *In secntd grad I wold like to lren*
> *times and divigine becos I like to*
> *learn all lot.*
> *(August 12)*

Multiplication and division are advanced topics not usually emphasized in second grade.

Maricar Writes Independently and at Her Own Pace
Maricar had one quality that fit right in with the concept of writing workshop: She worked independently. Early in the year she didn't request help in spelling or in topic selection from me or her teammates. However, before I commenced writing workshop I noticed she was one of the slowest writers I had ever encountered and that she often stayed in the classroom to finish assigned writings.

After writing workshop began, the length of time students wrote varied from twenty minutes to forty-five minutes. They wrote with what I call their "home" or "working" team, groups of four students formed randomly and changed every twelve weeks.

At the beginning of the year, we began the writing sessions simply by passing out writing folders. Students started new stories, continued drafts, or worked on illustrations, engaging in lots of conversation and movement as they discussed their stories, sharpened pencils, and got materials. A number of students complained that it was too noisy to write. When I asked the class to reflect on how we could improve writing workshop, Maricar, the independent worker, wrote:

> *I think people should stop talking. Becase we can't consatrate (concentrate).*
> *(October 29)*

For the rest of the year we began our writing sessions with five quiet minutes or, as students often called it, "five minutes peace." After getting their writing folders and materials, everyone (including myself) worked for five minutes in silence. Following this, students were free to talk in quiet voices and move around the classroom. I found that beginning writing workshop in this way often set the tone for a more productive writing session.

Maricar's first efforts in writing workshop were slow and tentative:

> *Once upon a time There was a Rabbit the rabbit aets (eats) crits (carrots) and lives inside the caige and it drigs (drinks) watir (water).*
> *(August 22)*

When asked to write about what she thought of writing workshop in early October, she said she didn't like it "becase we write too much." Her early stories were brief and included little detail. It took several days each to complete her first pieces of writing. In four of her first five stories, Maricar used a simple "I like ____ because ____" pattern somewhere in her story. This was not a pattern that I talked about or encouraged. Other stories were little more than short lists. She began each story with a capital letter and often included only one period — at the end. She did not use titles but, starting in late October, began to include "The End" in some stories. She did not talk to other students during the writing sessions, and her first five stories had no pictures. This was perplexing, because in my experience immature writers often depend on pictures to tell their stories.

In early October Maricar used a strategy that she would use at other times during the year — writing multiple stories about the same topic. She took the structure and theme of a previous story, changed a few words, added some details and demonstrated more control over the use of a particular skill. In Maricar's fifth story, she returned to a recently-used Christmas theme but composed a new story that included more appropriate use of periods:

> *In christmas we cold open prisits (presents) and sing christmas sogs (songs) I like christmas becous I get a lote of toys.*
> *(August 28)*

> *I lik Christmas because we can open print(presents) And play whit(with) thme(them). In Christmas i had a calculator. I use it whin(when) I whnt (want) to.*
> *The End*
> *(October 8)*

I should point out that Maricar's use of periods did not consistently improve over the course of the year. Her writing exhibited times of growth punctuated by regression — an example of the recursive nature of the writing process.

In mid-February Maricar had a breakthrough. She worked for two weeks on a story prompted by an event in her life. I observed her grinding out this story day by day, line by line, pretty much in silence. She made frequent use of her spelling handbook, which contained lists of high-frequency words. There were times I wondered if she would ever finish, but she did:

> *Last Friday my mom's car got hit and my mom and my sister woke up and looked out side and my hole faumaly woke up and we all went out side and then the polies man went to our house and talked to my mom and to the person who hit my mom's car. And my mom told me to chang my cloesd (clothes) and go to school and my sister went in side the house and whached (watched) tv my sister wacted (watched) cartoon's and my grandma was sitting downe and my grandepa was sitting downe to. And my mom brote (brought) me to school and my mom went to work and gose (goes) home at nigthe (night) and my mom called my dad and told what hapende (happened).*
> *The End*
> *(February 18)*

Maricar's story was the most detailed example of a personal incident story to appear in our writing workshop up to this time. In fact, few students had chosen to write such stories. When Maricar, who by now was participating in author's chair, shared this story I sensed heightened interest from the class. She conducted a lively response session, with many questions and comments. As to why the class seemed to particularly enjoy this story, Maricar wrote in her journal: "I think they liked it because it is ture (true)." We were all learning more about our quietest student.

In this story Maricar demonstrates her first use of the apostrophe in both possessive nouns (mom's) and contractions (did't). She also over-generalizes its use incorrectly in a plural noun (cartoon's), but what's important is that Maricar did this on her own. We had not discussed apostrophes in mini-lessons yet, and those students using apostrophes at this time were generally more mature writers.

In March Maricar wrote a sequel to her "accident" story. It is an even better example of the strategy I discussed earlier in which she returns to a topic and improves the use of a particular skill. Here she demonstrates growth in the use of periods and capital letters, dealing in this short story both with a familiar topic and fewer sentences in which she can attend more to mechanics:

> *Next Monday we are going to get my mom's new car. The car is called a Honda. My mom's car doesn't have a radiyo. And it dose'nt have a air condisoner. My mom wants to buy a radiyo. My mom wanted a red car but they did'int have that color.*
> *(March 9)*

In my journal I wrote, "The variety of her topics, increasing length of stories and perseverance on stories over time make me upgrade her from below average to average writer when compared to the class." I now stopped worrying about how long it took Maricar to complete stories; now I started trusting her pace and rhythm. However, when I asked the class to reflect in their journals about who was a good writer in this class and why, nobody mentioned Maricar.

Maricar's Reluctance at Author's Chair Turns to Enthusiasm

In writing workshop, students had regular opportunities to share their writing in author's chair. This was a public performance, one of the sort that a shy person like Maricar might want to avoid. Initially everyone who had a completed draft could read aloud. A slow trickle of students reading aloud soon turned into a stampede with some very long author's chairs. These sessions did not include listener feedback. Maricar did not share her writing during these sessions.

In October, as enthusiasm for author's chair was getting out of hand, I instituted a sign-up sheet for this activity and placed a limit of two authors each day so students could get feedback on their writing from the audience. On October 30th I noted in my journal, "I was surprised that Maricar shared today. She read with a great deal of confidence." In November Maricar shared again and I noted, "The quiet voices are starting to be heard in author's chair. Maricar is changing."

Other than that, I didn't notice any changes in Maricar's quiet reserved behavior. While Maricar rarely volunteered to give other students feedback, she seemed to enjoy the questions students asked her. When comparing the old author's chair (no feedback) with the new author's chair, Maricar wrote in her writing workshop journal:

> *I like the new one because we only do 2 at a time and the addnt (audience) get to ask you quscens and you have to answer and it bettr than the old one.*
> *(December 19)*

Maricar became a regular participant in author's chair. Her confidence grew throughout the year. She read in a strong voice and had the ability to focus the audience's attention even though she read with little expression. She seemed to enjoy answering questions about herself and her writing. Author's chair gave her a chance to be in the spotlight without seeking it out.

Maricar's Ability to Listen Benefits Herself and Others
One can not talk and listen at the same time, and the quiet Maricar learned by listening. As a good listener she tried out

some of the ideas introduced by her classmates. Maricar's writing was influenced by the stories and poems shared daily by her peers. She responded to some topics and trends that became popular in the class and were prominent in stories shared during author's chair.

When students in author's chair started ending their stories with "That's all folks" or "Sorry kids, that's all folks" Maricar tried using such endings, and toward the end of the year, when titles like "The Three Princes," "The Three Bears," and "The Three Friends" appeared, Maricar followed by writing "The Three Princesses" and "The Three Mermaids." Further, when many "Cookie's Week" pattern stories were shared in author's chair following my reading of a new class library book titled *Cookie's Week* by Cindy Ward, Maricar followed by writing her own story:

> *Cooke's (Cookie's) Week*
> *On Monday cooke went to school. on Tuesday cooke went out side to play wihe (with) his firends (friends). On Wenday cooke went to the refgratr (refrigerator) and he got a cold. And he sied (said) that he wold (would) never open the refgratr ever agin (again). The End*
> *(February 13)*

Because I wanted my students to share writing more often, I set up small student-led response groups. One group met each day while the rest of the class wrote. The response group format allowed other students to benefit from Maricar's willingness to listen. For many students, including Maricar, sharing in author's chair seemed to spur them to work a bit faster on stories. In response groups they could read their drafts and respond to each other's work. These groups allowed students who avoided author's chair, a group that did not now include Maricar, to read regularly in a small group setting.

In her group, called The Rainbow Club, Maricar was always on task. She was an excellent listener, asking specific questions that helped draw out more of each story, as with Gary's story, "The Kind Pig":

Maricar: *Any picture?*

Gary: *Here's your picture dudes.*

Maricar: *Why did Maria go to Joshua's house?*

Gary: *Because she wanted to go there.*

Marco: *Why did Joshua ask Maria to spend the night at the house?*

Gary: *Because he is scared of the dark.*

Maricar: *How old is Maria?*

Gary: *Six years old.*

Marco: *Why is he scared of the dark?*

Gary: *Because he thinks there's a giant tarantula in the room because of the clothes in the closet.*

Maricar: *Is Joshua always scared of the dark?*

Gary: *Yes.*

Maricar: *What about Maria, is she scared of the dark?*

Gary: *No.*

As Maricar's relationship with her response group evolved, she became more than a careful listener and questioner, becoming now more assertive. Students sometimes prematurely announced "Finished!" to end response group work. But Maricar would counter with, "Any questions for me?" or, "No, Gary didn't ask me a question."

At times response groups could turn silly, with students asking irrelevant questions or making funny comments. In the following exchange Egda tries to get Maricar off track by asking her for the ages of characters not in her story. Maricar remains firm about her story, "Mrs. Rabbit":

> Egda: *How old were the mother kangaroo and baby kangaroo? (The other students in the group were laughing.)*
>
> Maricar: *I don't have them in my story.*
>
> Egda: *But what are their ages?*
>
> Maricar: *I don't have them in my story.*
>
> *(The group then continued with more appropriate questions.)*

In February, when I was debating whether or not to continue having response groups because of the increased noise level in the classroom, Maricar argued to keep them:

> *I think response groups are good because I like to read. And I think we sould have response groups so we can learn how to read.*
> *(February 28)*

When I asked the class near the end of the year to advise me about whether to have response groups next year, Maricar was one of only two students who commented that response groups could help with revision:

> *I think you sould keep on having response grops because that person could add new things to his or her story after the response grop.*
> *(July 24)*

In the small group setting, Maricar was much more motivated to ask questions than in the author's chair setting. Perhaps one reason for this was that she was not as caught up in the need to show herself off as were some others. Therefore, in the response group Maricar listened and contributed more to other students than many of her classmates.

Finally, Maricar benefited from attentive listening during my mini-lessons. Every day, either at the beginning or end of writing workshop, the class assembled on the carpet for a five to fifteen-minute lesson planned on needs I perceived from observation and from my own knowledge of writing and young writers. On some days we would simply read and enjoy books from our class library. On others we would discuss the works of a special author, one we might study over a long period. We spent many of these lessons brainstorming ideas for topics, titles, story starters, endings and problems to include in our stories. We discussed skills — spelling, grammar, and punctuation. We read and evaluated writing of student authors from sources outside our classroom. Often students shared what they were doing that day.

During the mini-lessons Maricar sat quietly, well behaved and often stone-faced. Her large dark brown eyes rarely wandered from their attentive focus on me. In whole group discussions, Maricar did not share ideas unless I called on her or everyone was required to respond, as when we sat in a circle and had a quick check-in about the status of everyone's writing. While I at times was frustrated with Maricar's lack of participation during group discussion, over time I learned that she was in fact listening attentively and was unusually receptive to the content of the mini-lessons, as she demonstrated in her writing. Here is an example of how she learned by listening.

About three weeks after we finished studying the work of Marc Brown (particularly his series of Arthur books), Maricar began writing her own series of Arthur stories. Shortly after finishing Brown's stories, I gave a lesson on story starters such as, "One day" and "Once upon a time." These forms turned up in Maricar's next stories:

Peggy Ate Arthur
One day Arthur was walking to shcool (school) whin (when)
a pig whint (went) by and try to aet (eat) arthur but arthur
run so fast the pig codln't (couldn't) cahe (catch) up thin
arthur run to school. The End.
(October 29)

Arthur and the tooht (tooth)
Once upon a time Arthur was at school whan he tih (tried)
moveing his teeth and his teeth was moveing he pool it out
and wasen't liesaneg (listening) to the teacher the teacher
calld arthur the teacher tollde (told) arthur to liesan arthur
to wahs (wash) it and wene he got home from school and
arthur put his tooth under his piowwle (pillow) and he got $5.
(November 15)

In addition to incorporating the story starters, Maricar's last "Arthur" story is longer and more detailed than anything she had written to that point and contains some indirect dialogue. "Like a butterfly emerging from its chrysalis," I wrote in my journal, "Maricar too is going through her own stages of growth. She slowly looks, talks and acts more like a writer. She plodded early in the year but now her confidence appears to be soaring."

Later, two of our mini-lessons focused on writing about family members, particularly siblings. I read a number of "family" stories I had saved from former students throughout the years.

Many of those stories were about brothers and sisters annoying the writer. The mini-lessons ended with a suggestion to write about a brother or sister. Maricar immediately followed with this story:

> *My younger sister*
> *When ever my younger sister goes to my grandmas house*
> *and when I whath (watch) tv my younger sister*
> *canches (changes) canel (channel) and I have to whath what*
> *she whathes. The End*
> *(February 24)*

Maricar didn't respond in her writing to all mini-lessons; she very much picked and chose what appealed or made sense to her. That was what I had hoped for, and I was pleased to see how often she responded by using material that had been presented in the mini-lessons. If her grade had been based only on her responses to mini-lessons, she would have been an "A" student.

Writing Workshop Provides a Way for Maricar to Connect with Other Students

At the end of February Maricar began writing her first story with "friends" as the theme. "My Best Friends" was not much more than a listing of her best friends and a few details about play at recess. In it Maricar listed all of the girls in the class as her best friends, although I rarely observed her playing at recess with anyone, nor do I think any of the girls she mentioned would have listed her as their best friend. I think that this story, along with additional "friends" stories that would soon follow, presented Maricar's yearning to be a more integral part of the social fabric of the class.

In addition, Maricar spent about a week and a half drawing tiny, detailed pictures of her eleven "best friends," with names identifying each girl. In this picture, Maricar is surrounded by the girls while the three most popular girls in the class (Kristine, Liza, and Kimberly) jump rope. These three outgoing girls had been classmates of Maricar in kindergarten and first grade; they were confident writers who often collaborated with each other on detailed chapter stories.

In April, Maricar continued her "friends" theme by beginning a string of four stories in which students, particularly the more popular girls, played a prominent role as characters. One student, Liza, appeared in all four stories. She was a leader in the class (both academically and socially), and I believe it was Maricar's desire to be more involved with Liza and the other popular girls that motivated her new direction. Although most students who write about friends usually place themselves in a central role in the story, Maricar didn't include herself in any of these stories:

> *The Three Pricss (Princesses)*
> *Once upon a time ther were three pricss named Liza, Kimberly and Sarah. And they were best friends. And they went to school togeter. And they play togeter. And they did everyting togeter. And there favorite game to play is 4 Coners (Corners). And there seconed best game to play is 2 seqwer (square). And there thered (third) best game to play is soccer. And there fout (fourth) best game to play is cinese jumprope. The End.*
> *(April 8)*

In Maricar's next story, which is longer, Liza, Sarah, and Fran are swimming together and get scared by a turtle. They summon three "guys" who help them by getting the turtle out of the sea:

> *Once upon a time there where (were) three mermaids and ther name's where Liza, Sarah, and Fran. They like to swim*

togetor. And they saw a little turtle and they got scerd. Thn they went out and called for help. And three guys. Named Mikel and Mathue and Rommel. Help Liza and Sarah and Fran first they told them that there was a turtle in the sea. Then Rommel got the turle out of the sea so the three mermaids went back to the sea and played Hide-and-go-seek Fran was it and Liza and Sarah was hideing in the backyard and Fran found them. And when they wear (were) done playing they went to Liza's house and got some milk and cookies. And after that they wear (were) done playing theu went to Liza's house and got soem milk and cookies. And after that they wear done ateing (eating) there snak (snack) tey will go swimming in the swimming pool. The End. (April 14)

In May Maricar found herself in a new working team with Kristine, one of the most popular girls in the class. Kristine appeared as a character in Maricar's next two stories, "Liza and Her Friends" and the "Three Missing Girls." "Liza and Her Friends" took Maricar three weeks to write and was her longest story of the year. When Maricar shared this story in author's chair, she received positive feedback from the students whose names she used. They beamed when Maricar read their names and they were the first to raise their hands for responses.

I sensed that Kristine, who now sat across form Maricar, pulled Maricar more into her social and writing workshop worlds. Occasionally they talked quietly and read their writing to each other. Once I heard Kristine ask Maricar to put her in a story. Kristine was often surrounded by many of the more popular girls, who came to her desk to talk about her writing. Her most regular visitors, Liza and Kimberly (both Filipinas), often collaborated with Kristine on complex chapter stories that they regularly read during author's chair. Maricar visited Liza at her working team, where she helped Maricar with spelling. Maricar also talked with Geno, who was in her working team. Maricar, he said, helped him get ideas for stories and characters.

Maricar and Kristine spent the last week and a half of school collaborating on stories about each other at Kristine's suggestion. They worked together by asking each other questions and writing their responses in the form of an "All About _____ Story," a format we had worked on earlier in the year. Kristine completed her story very rapidly — within two days — and although she then moved on to something else, Maricar continued to ask Kristine questions and write her story. This was the only time during the year that Maricar worked with a partner on a story. Maricar was indeed changing, losing some of her "phantom" characteristics through her interest in writing, which in turn led to increased interaction with her fellow students:

All About Kristine
Kristine's last name is Isip.
Kristine's favorite food is senigang.
Kristine's favorite color is purple and read and pink and yellow and black and brown and green and oreng.
Kristine like pizza. Kristine's best friend is Liza.
The End
(July 15)

All About Maricar
Maricar likes pupies. Her best friend is Liza, Kristine, Fran, Sarah, Sophia, Karla, Kimberly, and Maria. Her very best friend is Liza. Maricar's faverit color is red and purple. When Maricar grows up she wants to be a doctor. She likes going to the moole (mall). Her best park she likes to go to is Glen Cove Park. She has a sister and her name is Kamille. Maricar will be 8 on August 9.

The story Maricar was preparing to begin as the year came to an end was titled "Liza and Kristine," the names of the two most popular students in the class. Everyday now Maricar was looking more beyond herself, more to her peers.

Conclusion
My writing has changed because my writing is better and my drawing is better and my writing is getting longer. (July 27)

My case-study in the context of writing workshop has led me to appreciate Glenda Bissex's remark:

> *Case-study research is directed largely toward understanding; such descriptive research requires us to suspend judgment and just look. Researching in this way can be transforming because it changes the way we see others and ourselves.*

I saw that:

1. Writing workshop worked for Maricar because it was ordered, structured and predictable. As one of my colleagues said, the workshop provided "a safe haven for a shy student."

2. Writing workshop allowed Maricar to work at her own pace. Maricar was not limited by the very slow speed at which she wrote. I often wonder how I would have perceived Maricar's writing if I had only seen her write on teacher-assigned topics that had to be completed in a forty-five minute period.

    Early in the year I had worried about Maricar's ability to work in an environment that required a great deal of independence because she was a slower writer, but over the year it became clear that she had found a way to challenge herself and show steady growth.

3. Writing workshop gave Maricar a chance to choose her topics. Her greatest leap forward as a writer came when she narrated a family crisis. Writing workshop gives all students an opportunity to focus on what is important in their lives, but quiet students who are not so verbal and demonstrative may particularly benefit from this freedom.

4. Writing workshop called on one of Maricar's greatest strengths: her ability to listen. Although in large groups Maricar did not have much to say, she benefited from what she heard, and the results showed in her writing. A quiet student can be learning even if she is not contributing to discussions.

5. Besides providing an environment where Maricar could develop as a writer, writing workshop also allowed her to become more integrated into the social fabric of the classroom. Although still very much a loner out on the playground, by the end of the year she was becoming less isolated in the classroom; she was slowly beginning to collaborate with other students, and her use of other students as characters in the stories she was writing during the last part of the school year was winning the attention and approval of students whom Maricar longed to have as friends.

Final Thoughts

If Maricar responded to the predictable nature of writing workshop by feeling more secure and confident, I must question the way I teach in other curriculum areas where I do not have such predictable structures. I want to explore moving towards the use of more "workshops" in my classroom — in reading, in science, and in art. I want to find ways to involve my students in long-term projects in all subject areas. Maricar taught me the value in giving students the opportunity to pick up where they left off the previous day.

By looking closely at Maricar I found much to respect, admire and expect from quiet students. She taught me that a student who is extremely reserved in whole group discussions and inter-actions with peers can excel and even show leadership skills in other formats where talk is required. My own senses are now sharpened, expecting to hear from quiet students, but knowing that I can only hear if I listen closely and provide a variety of opportunities for talk to occur.

At the beginning of the year I viewed Maricar as an immature writer, but as I studied her more closely this view changed. By the end of the school year, I saw her as an above average/ad-vanced writer. At the same time, my view of what successful writers do was changing, and I was including more factors in evaluating my students as writers. I began to see Maricar as a complex writer. She had variety in her stories, took risks in both her spelling and topic choice, had an extraordinary ability to stick with stories over a long period of time, edited and revised her writing and was unusually responsive to both mini-lessons and her peers. Like all good writers, she was actively involved, processing what was occurring in our writing workshop and integrating much of that learning into her writing.

While I learned much from my research project, I feel that I am just beginning to understand the quiet side of my classroom.

In an interview with the *San Francisco Chronicle*, film maker Jim Jarmusch speaks of his approach to making a film which emphasizes life's "insignificant details":

"Maybe it's the spaces in between, those moments we don't think about, that really shape our lives." I came on this quote before I started my research and more and more I came to see that, for me, the phantom student was one of the spaces in between. I am left wondering what other in between spaces exist in my work. This project has been one significant step as I continue my teaching journey, always learning more about my students and my craft.

References

Bissex, G. (1987). Why case studies? In R. Bullock (Ed.), *Seeing for ourselves : Case study research by teachers of writing* (pp. 7-19). Portsmouth, NH: Heinemann.

Graves, D. (1983). *Writing: Teachers and children at work.* Exeter, NH: Heinemann.

Ward, C. (1988). *Cookie's week.* New York: G. P. Putnam's Sons.

No Problem. We Can Speak with the Hands:

Group Work in a Sheltered High School Classroom

by

MYRON BERKMAN

There's something magical about conversation at this school. The ethnic mix brings an instant spark. Learning goes on every instant; every interaction is a new experience. To get a project completed, students must negotiate with each other. And because they are all newcomers to the U. S., and from different countries, English is their only common medium. (Teacher Journal Entry)

FOR the past twelve years I have taught at Newcomer High School in San Francisco, a unique school dedicated to teaching recently-arrived immigrant and refugee youth from around the world. There are no native English speakers in the school. The majority of students have had seven years or less of education in their country and represent a wide range of ethnic diversity. As of 1994, the largest ethnic groups were Central American, Chinese, Vietnamese, Russian, and Filipino.

Newcomer serves as a port of orientation for these students to both the school system and the United States. Students generally spend one year at the school before they go on to regular high schools. Although they will probably receive English As a Second Language (ESL) instruction in the regular high schools, we do as much as we can in this introductory first year to prepare them to enter the American school system and American culture.

The students study ESL half the day, and then receive bilingual instruction in math and social studies. Currently, bilingual instruction is offered in Tagalog, Chinese, Spanish, and Vietnamese.

Students who speak other languages, such as Arabic, Korean, or Lao, or whose schedules do not allow them to study in a bilingual class, study social studies and math in "Sheltered Social Studies" classes. The content is taught in English, using ESL techniques and strategies emphasizing visuals, gestures, and slower speech — all the things Stephen Krashen calls "comprehensible input."

Over the past few years I have taught a Sheltered Social Studies class called San Francisco Perspectives. In the class students are introduced to American culture and geography using San Francisco and the Bay Area as the context. The students' educational backgrounds have been as varied as their linguistic backgrounds. Some students know virtually no English, while others have studied English for three or four years in their native countries. Students work on three or four major group projects over the semester, investigating different schools and communities in San Francisco and California. Working in groups of three or four, they put together multimedia projects involving research, art, interviews, and photographs. Each student is responsible for specific tasks. Through these groups, I've worked to create a "community of learners" in the classroom, an environment where the teacher and the students are learning from each other.

These group projects came to mind when, as a member of the Urban Sites Network, I began to take an interest in classroom research. From 1991 to 1993, nine other Bay Area classroom teachers and I, meeting monthly, started writing and talking feverishly about our classrooms, beginning a headlong thrust into the field of teacher inquiry.

I chose to look at the group projects because, despite what I judged as the success of this technique, there was much about the dynamics of what was going on that I did not know. Students were submitting beautiful 20-30 page reports, full of good writing, art work, and photographs. I thought the projects were successful, but what did the students think? What were they really learning? What was going on in their groups as they put their projects together?

These questions served as a springboard into my research. I decided to focus on the student work in the different groups to see what I could find. I was interested in what kind of groups worked best. Homogeneous groups? Mixed language groups? Random groups? I decided to collect artifacts from the group projects to see what I could find. These included writing samples, student reflection logs, classroom observations, and individual and group interviews. As I began to collect these artifacts, I quickly realized that it would be impossible to look at all the students' work closely.

At my school site, I was involved in another project, the HERALD Project, which focused on interdisciplinary teaching and teacher reflection. An English teacher, a science teacher and I decided to look at our students from a cross-disciplinary perspective. Because of scheduling problems, there were very few students that we all had in common. But there was one Mexican girl, Marisol, who was in all our classes. We all decided to use her as our target student. Rather than make more work for myself, I decided to use Marisol for both projects and to begin tracing her language growth over the course of a semester.

The vehicle for tracing the growth would be the group projects. As evidence, I wanted to chart her work in three different groups: a homogeneous primary language group, a heterogeneous mixed language group, and finally a self-selected group. I hoped to be able to study Marisol's learning in these different group environments and also, looking through Marisol's eyes, take a closer look at the group projects to see if the processes were as valuable as the products were impressive.

But there was another goal which emerged over the course of my inquiry. And that was related to my own learning. I wanted to see what this close look at one student would do for me, the teacher. What could I learn from this exacting look at one student that would help my teaching?

Marisol: "I Was Thinking in Spanish, and Then Writing the Content in English"

Marisol appeared in class in September with an infectious smile and a lack of shyness which differentiated her from most of the recently arrived Newcomer students. She had dark brown eyes and medium length brown hair which covered her forehead with bangs. What I remember most was her laugh. She would throw back her head and out would come something between a giggle and a laugh. When I asked questions in class that first week, she was one of the few who would dare to answer. Her confidence stood out. She was not afraid to make a mistake in English. If she was wrong, she would try again. And to both my dismay and delight, she would often argue with me if I told her she was wrong.

This contrasted with most of the other ESL students in the class. It would sometimes take them weeks or even months before they would gain the confidence to begin to speak English in class. Most of their utterances would be limited to one-word answers or short phrases. But not Marisol. She was ready to speak.

She told me she had studied some English in Mexico. Her mother was a lawyer in Mexico and had sent her to live with Marisol's older sister in San Francisco. In a survey she had taken in another class, Marisol had written that she read a lot in Mexico, both at home and in school. From all this information we can see that Marisol had distinct advantages over most of the students. It appeared that she came from a home environment that valued education and literacy. She was quite literate in Spanish. Most students at our school don't come with these same advantages. Many come from families that are semi or non-literate in their own language. Very few of them live in home environments where English is spoken.

During the first week of school, I asked the students to write about their countries. Marisol wrote:

> *In Mexico the school is good because all the people have the chance for study in public school or private, the schools are big, have for about 30 classroom.*

> *All the schools have students bads, and good, with the bads students the teachers goes with they a the office. When study more time.*

> *...the clothes are uniforms, for the girls ... third grade is light red with a white skirts, and shoes black...*

From the very beginning Marisol was not afraid to give her opinion. She began by writing about schools and choice, and good and bad students. She tells the reader that the bad students have detention if they misbehave:

> *...with the bad students, the teacher goes with they a the office. When study more time.*

Errors like "students bads" and "shoes black" are common for Spanish-speaking students. They derive from the Spanish placement of nouns before adjectives. Compared to other students in my class, this was good writing. Most students wrote very basic information about their school, such as "My school is big. I like school."

Reflecting on this first writing a year later, Marisol told me that she felt most of her mistakes were from Spanish. "I was thinking in Spanish and then writing the content in English." She pointed out that "have the choice for study" was directly translated from the Spanish "para estudiar." Thinking in their first language and then attempting to directly translate into English is a common strategy for beginning ESL students.

But what was most important to me was that while there were many errors, I could hear a voice struggling to tell me what she thought about schools. Unlike many students who simply gave basic information and rattled off the lists of subjects studied, Marisol wanted the reader to know that Mexican students had a choice in their education. Her emphasis was on communication, not grammar. This emphasis on communication over the course of the semester proved to be Marisol's strongest asset as an ESL learner.

Group Project #1, Homogeneous Groups: "I Think So, but the Teacher Tell Me, That I Wrote from the Book." In November Marisol worked on her first full-fledged group project, involving three other students. Her group prepared a report on North Beach, a neighborhood in San Francisco we had visited on a field trip. In this project, I grouped the students by native language, so that Marisol was grouped with three other Spanish-speaking students. Because it was early in the year, I wanted them to feel comfortable using their primary language. My belief is that for most students this security is essential in getting students to feel okay about themselves in order to begin adapting fully to their new language and culture. Once this sense of ease is achieved, I believe their learning of English will come more easily.

In this project Marisol and her three classmates worked together to produce a report about the neighborhood that included photographs, research, maps and interviews. Marisol's responsibility for the project was to write about the photographs the group took on the field trip. Under one of the photographs she had written:

> *This picture is from North Beach. It's a district with a colorful past one which encompasses the Barbary Coast tradition. Successive waves of immigrants have left their mark on North Beach. Currently, the are is predominantly Italian...*

> *It's safe and great neighborhood for walking with lots of Italian cafes where cappuccino, enticing lunches and scrumptious pastries may be found. ... Italian bakeries are bulging with homemade bread and sinfully rich pastries such.*

I suspected that some of these terms had been copied from a brochure she picked up during the field trip. Words like "predominant," and "successive waves," just don't fit with the voice of a beginning-level ESL student. I gave her a "B" on the project but wrote in my evaluation of her report that some parts of the writing sounded like they had been copied, and I was looking more for her own words.

After the project was completed, students were asked to complete a reflection log, focusing on such questions as, "What did you learn from this project?" "What was the most difficult thing about the project?" and "What did you learn from your partners?" I thought it was important that they began to think about how they were learning. Marisol's reflection log contained this response to the question, "Is your writing better now than it was when you were working on the last project?":

> *I don't know. I think so, but the teacher tell me, that I wrote from the book!*

Well … I could feel the steam rising from her pen. Marisol was indignant. The exclamation point after the word "book" showed how hurt she was. In fact, she wouldn't speak to me for several days. But I was pleased to see her confidence in revealing her anger to me. Most ESL students never dare show their anger to the teacher. They are either too concerned that it will affect their grade, or they hold the teacher in such high reverence that they wouldn't dare speak out in opposition.

But Marisol wasn't afraid. And she could even display that anger in writing. Again I saw voice and power in her writing. I could hear Marisol's inner conversation: "I think I am writing better. But apparently the teacher doesn't agree. He thinks I am copying." Her sharp retort to me also showed me signs of progress in her writing. Her spelling was improved. Aside from a mistake in the past tense, "tell" for "told," the writing was much better than her last project. She was moving away from simple sentences like "there are good students and bad" and was now using clauses like "that wrote from the book."

To Marisol, simply lifting a couple of sentences out of a pamphlet was not copying. And besides, there were other parts of the report where she had contributed much of her own writing. In another portion she had tried to integrate some of the writing in the book or pamphlet into her own ideas:

> *This neighborhood is the most important of business. The most of people come to Downtown of shopping, Downtown has many stores like, Macy's, Northroom, Limited, in fact many kinds of stores.*

The writing in this paragraph contrasted sharply with the "successive waves of immigrants" writing. It was clear she had lifted some pages out of the book. But perhaps I had erred in not mentioning the good parts of her writing that had been authentic and clear. In Marisol's mind I was saying she had copied all her report, and she certainly hadn't.

Marisol later told me that this project had been very frustrating for her. Her partners were supposed to have collected information to give to her so she could write it up in the final report. But she said, "They didn't help me. Alejandro didn't do his job, getting information about the pictures. I was angry." As to my charge of copying, "I didn't know how to put it in my words. I understood it. I only copied two sentences."

As we spoke more, I began to understand that it had been a matter of pride. She felt hurt. Especially because she felt that the others had not done their jobs. She felt she was being un-fairly penalized by only getting a "B."

I learned more about Marisol's thinking about grouping from her reflection log. In her evaluation she seemed unhappy with her group. Her answer to the question, "What did you learn from your partners?" was blunt: "Nothing. Some of my group help me with the information of some neighborhoods." When asked if she liked working with partners, she wrote, "Yes, when they are organizate and if they want to work."

Even though all the students in Marisol's group spoke Spanish, their educational backgrounds were quite different. Jimmy, a Spanish-speaking Chinese student from Puerto Rico, attended class sporadically. Mart, although Mexican like Marisol, spoke very little English and had less schooling in Mexico.

Here I got a clear indication of Marisol's thinking about groups. It didn't matter what language they spoke. What was important to Marisol was how well they worked and whether they wanted to work. In other words, I believe Marisol was saying, "Yes, I like group work, if the other members do their share." The problem in this project had been that Marisol felt that the other group members had not done what they were assigned to do.

When I originally assigned the reflection logs after each assign-ment, I really wasn't sure of their value. Here already in the second assignment I learned some valuable lessons from Marisol's reflections. Just because everyone spoke the same language did not automatically make it easier for the group. Factors like edu-cational background, years of English studied, and personality were just as important as native language.

Group Project #2, Heterogeneous Groups:
"Igor, You Have to Put This in Paragraph"

A few weeks later in the next project, Marisol was grouped with a Korean, a Russian, and an El Salvadoran. Their task was to go out and investigate another neighborhood in San Francisco, the Seacliff district. Marisol and her partners decided who would be responsible for the various assignments. These included taking photographs, researching the neighborhood history, making a map, and conducting an interview with a neighborhood resident. After two weeks of hard work, the group turned in a very thorough 25-page report complete with all the above components. The project received an "A" grade.

As part of the project, students were asked to state their individual contributions. Marisol's major responsibility was to conduct the interview. Alejandro took the photographs, Igor wrote the history of the neighborhood, and Min Yong did the map. Marisol wrote:

> *Well, in this project about the neighborhoods. I did the I copied the interview. I copied the answered on the paper, then I had to do the transcription. clear of questions and answers. I helped to Igor do the story about Seacliff, he wrote the story about Seacliff, he wrote the story and I just wrote in paragraphs, to correct some words and put more information in it. I helped to Min Yong to do the map putting some names of the places and colored, I wrote the information from an encyclopedia about Seacliff.*

It appeared she had done a lot of work and learned a lot. But I still had many questions. What processes did Marisol use to do this writing? Did working in the group help her writing at all? How did Marisol feel about working with a mixed-language group as opposed to her previous Spanish-speaking group? And,

I wondered, did they really get any work done during their group time together, or were they just fooling around? I decided to take a close look at this group and see if any of my questions could be answered.

During the project I had recorded one of their group meetings a few days before the project was due. I had urged each group to use their time together to make sure all the components were included in their report: research, maps, photographs, and interviews. I also wanted them to proofread their writing and check for paragraphs. One of the hardest tasks for ESL students is learning to write in paragraphs. They often hand in one or two page reports comprised of one or two long paragraphs. I tried to convey the idea that each new paragraph should contain a new topic. These students would be exiting into a regular high school in two or three months. In order to pass their proficiency exams and succeed in their classes, they had to know how to write a paragraph.

What follows is a partial transcript from a group meeting about two days before the project deadline. I asked a classroom volunteer to tape the group. The group began by introducing themselves:

> Igor: *My name is Igor. I'm the writer in this group. In this project I write story about Seacliff. We went to Seacliff in Saturday, March 16. In this project I write story, plan of group, and I went to library and took information about Seacliff.*
>
> Min Yong: *My name is Min Yong. I made the map so I . . . I . . . the map.*
>
> Marisol: *(her speed and delivery are about five times faster than the rest of her group.) O.K. My name is Marisol. I did the interview. I . . . uh . . . got some person of the Seacliff, and I asked the 10 questions.*

Alejandro: *Mi nombre es Alejandro Teran.*

Marisol: *En Ingles! (Marisol translates) ... He's Alejandro. He take a picture of the Seacliff, the people, the museum, interesting places of Seacliff. He take a picture, Golden Gate Bridge. His last name? Teran. Teran.*

Right away Marisol took over. I wasn't sure if it was because her English was better than the others, or if it was because of her outgoing personality. Both Alejandro and Min Yong had recently transferred into the class and were still rather shy and reluctant to speak. Min Yong, at this point, moved over to an adjacent desk to work on a map of the neighborhood. Alejandro began putting the photographs in order on the floor:

Marisol: *The people who I interviewed say that some of the people live since 1924. So, the old people live 70 years. (Marisol then proceeds to read Igor's writing out loud.) "...On November 16, 1991, we had a field trip to Seacliff. This is nice beautiful neighborhood in San Francisco. Its boundaries are the 24th Avenue...." Igor, you have to put this in paragraph.*

Igor: *What?*

Marisol: *You have to put this, write in paragraph, you know? (Marisol repeats her instruction again, pausing after the words "this" and "write," so Igor will understand.)*

Marisol: *Like this. (She shows him a paragraph on a paper.)*

Igor: *You want to do it? O.K. Take homework. All the time you give me the papers for homework. (Igor is angry.) Paragraph. I know, I know. But it's difficult!*

Marisol: *Why is difficult? Only the difference you have to put in other ... you know? (She gestures at the paragraph.)*

Igor: *I know.*

Marisol: *Because the teacher is gonna say, you want to get this in paragraph.*

Igor: *O.K. I do it in home. It's my homework.*

(They continue to argue over who will do the revisions.)

Marisol: *Gimme this. I wanna read. (She takes back his report and continues reading.) "Many rich people live in Seacliff…"*

Igor: *Not true? The lady told us. Ask Mr. Berkman. Very nice house, you know? O.K. (He is trying to convince her that there are many rich people in the Seacliff.)*

Marisol: *(continues to read) "Many people lives." Why "s"?*

Igor: *Lives.*

Marisol: *Lives. Many people. Why you put "s"?*

Igor: *Ah … Yes. I… (Igor sees his error.)*

(Marisol is tired of arguing. She beckons teacher over.)

Marisol: *O.K. O.K. Teacher. This is okay? We have to put in paragraph?*

Teacher: *Always need paragraph.*

Marisol: *Igor! (She looks at Igor and laughs.)*

Igor: *Thank you, Marisol.*

Marisol: *You're welcome.*

(The teacher then reads their story and leaves saying, "Good. Try to get some paragraphs.")

Marisol: *Thank you. Do you know how to write "exactly"?*

Igor: *What?*

Marisol: *Do you know how to spell "exactly"?*

Igor: *Seacliff?*

Marisol: *"Exactly." (She says the word again for the third time.) Like this. (She writes down the word "exactly" and shows Igor.) You understand this?*

Igor: *Ah! Yes.*

Marisol: *Is right?*

Igor: *Yes.*

Marisol: *Because, some of, the my, no, no, no, because one of the, my questions I put "exactly," and I not sure is the spelling.*

Igor: *You can look on the ... dictionary, but no, I think it's good.*

Marisol: *O.K. Thank you. (Marisol begins speaking Spanish to Igor) Hola. Que Tal? Como tel allido: que bueno. Que estas haciendo su praeto? Entonces me allegro. Cuando van a ir manana? a donde?*

Igor: *Marisol. Many Spanish and you take "F."*

Marisol: *Why?*

Igor: *Because Mr. Berkman say.*

Marisol: *Why?*

Igor: *Because it's English lesson.*

Marisol continued to speak in Spanish. Igor countered by speaking in Russian. Soon their group was a hubbub of Spanish, Russian and Korean, and the meeting ended with Marisol and Min Yong singing gleefully, "Bessame Mucho" in Spanish.

This transcript revealed a wealth of information to me. First, I was delighted to see Marisol and the group on-task. Most of the time had indeed been spent going over the report, specifically discussing paragraphs and the "s" in third person singular.

During a normal class period, I usually walk around the room and observe and meet with different groups. I sometimes get the feeling that groups are fooling around much of the time. Focusing on this group gave me another perspective. The transcript showed they were on task, working with each other in the time allotted. Although they tailed off into their native languages at the end, this was understandable. After twenty minutes or so of an intense academic discussion in English, the group needed a break.

From the transcript we see that Min Yong and Alejandro, whose English levels were the lowest, said practically nothing. They went off to do other tasks. Both Min Yong and Alejandro had only been in the class a few weeks, and did not speak much in class. They might be characterized as being in Krashen's "pre-production stage." They are beginning speakers, not quite ready to "produce" speech. They can comprehend a little, and may be able to respond in short phrases, but they are not ready to partake in English conversations.

But Marisol was the leader here, and her confidence and strong communicative skills were evident right away. She read over Igor's material and immediately noticed the lack of paragraphs. "You have to put this … write in paragraph, you know?" The form is not great, but the message is clear. She slows down her speech and emphasizes the words "put this" and "write." She realizes that Igor might not understand "put this," so she rephrases it and says "write," to make sure he understands. And then she checks on him more to see if Igor understands by asking, "You know?"

Marisol wanted to be understood, and employed an array of strategies toward that end. She repeated things many times so that Igor would understand. She used nonverbal clues, waving her hands emphatically to make a point, and pointed to important parts of the paper she wanted Igor to look at. She was constantly listening and checking to see if her listener understood. Marisol was totally focused on communicating with Igor here. Form was secondary.

Marisol was offering what Krashen calls "comprehensible input," the extra-linguistic clues one must use to make oneself understood to someone who does not speak English as a first language. In fact, she demonstrated the very strategies I employ daily in my ESL classes.

But Marisol showed here that she was not only a communicator but a negotiator. She did not stand still, unbending. She acknowledged Igor's stand, and tried to work around his resistance. She sensed his anger about changing his writing when he responded, "You want to do it? OK. Take it!" So she adopted a more conciliatory tone, showing him that it was not a big deal, writing in paragraphs. It just involved changing things around a little bit. She saved her big trump card — the teacher — for the end. When she saw me within proximity, she called me over, and I unwittingly became a perfect accomplice to her cause by responding, "Always need paragraph."

But Marisol was not only a teacher here, she was also learning from Igor. When she was not sure about the spelling of "exactly," she turned to Igor for help. This was a nice reversal in light of the fact that just a minute before she had been the teacher, and Igor the student.

There was a rich discussion going on about language here. Marisol and Igor were having an extensive discussion on the use of third person singular and what constitutes a paragraph. Marisol reminded Igor that "many people" did not require an "s," many people "live" in the Seacliff. These issues are what Jim Cummins has called "Cognitive/Academic Language Proficiency" or CALP. Cummins makes distinctions between BICS (Basic Interpersonal Communicative Skills) and CALP. BICS describe the ability of a second language speaker to communicate in social interactions that are not cognitively demanding, while CALP refers to the second language speaker's ability to use the second language in an academic setting without contextual clues or visuals. Conversations which demand CALP are much more difficult for ESL students. Cummins maintains that the acquiring of CALP is a good predictor of success in a second language.

From this transcript we can see that Marisol and Igor were succeeding fairly well in discussing academic issues. And this discussion was made more difficult in that they were not just discussing the problem, but arguing. Arguing in a second language is difficult enough, but arguing about these language issues is even more difficult.

What is important here is that Igor and Marisol were so involved in their conversation that they were not focusing on speaking correctly. Although the focus of their discussion was on correct grammar or writing, in their conversation they were not thinking about being grammatically correct. They were having a rich conversation talking about academic issues, getting lots of CALP experience. They had an opportunity here to use some cognitively demanding language in a realistic situation.

Towards the end of this same project, I wanted to get Marisol's assessment of how she was doing. I called her over to my desk to ask her some questions:

Mr. Berkman: *Did you like this project?*

Marisol: *Yeah.*

Mr. Berkman: *Why?*

Marisol: *I ... I ... I can to meet the other neighborhoods of San Francisco and I like to meet, umm ... what kind of neighborhoods in San Francisco.*

Mr. Berkman: *How about your group? What do you think about your group?*

Marisol: *My group is good because uhh ... all the people work.*

Mr. Berkman: *Hmm. This group, well, Alejandro's Spanish, but you have a Russian, and a Korean. Is it a problem because they didn't speak English?*

Marisol: *No. Not is problem because we ... we can to speak with ... with the hands! (She laughs.) That's it. No is problem.*

Mr. Berkman: *In the last project you were with all Spanish (speaking) group, right? Which project was easier for you?*

Marisol: *This project.*

Mr. Berkman: *Really? Why? What about working with them? Was it harder or easier than the last project?*

Marisol: *No, easy. Both easy. (She says assuredly.)*

Mr. Berkman: *So it didn't make a difference for you that one group was all Spanish, and one group mixed?*

(Marisol nods in agreement.)

Mr. Berkman: *Did you learn anything from your partners?*

Marisol: *Yeah. How they work, how they thinking about, ummm, their form to work.*

I was surprised to hear that it was not a problem for Marisol to work in a mixed-language group. I had assumed that Marisol would prefer to work with students who spoke Spanish because they could speak freely and there would not be any linguistic problems. But Marisol reiterated to me that she didn't care whether or not her group was Spanish speaking; what was important to her was that they were willing to work hard.

Group Project #3: Student Choice — We Did the Best That We Could Do

It was getting toward the end of the semester and there was time for one final project. Since the entire class had been studying about California history, this time the students were free to work with whomever they wanted. In the first group project I had grouped Marisol in a Spanish speaking language group, and in the last project she had worked in a heterogeneous group with a Russian and a Korean. I wanted to see what kind of group Marisol would join if given a choice. I anticipated that she would group herself with other Spanish speakers. But Marisol and many other students in the class formed their groups based on factors other than just language.

Marisol formed a group with her friend Claudia from El Salvador, Brenda from Hong Kong and Liana from Armenia. They were all friends, but more importantly for Marisol, they were dependable and good students.

Marisol's group decided to do a report on Spanish California. Language was not a barrier for them. They did a terrific job, handing in a 46-page report, full of illustrations, maps, research and learning logs. Each student made valuable contributions to the report. Marisol's responsibilities were to write about the work and problems the Spanish faced in California. In her report she wrote:

...they learned to work from differents way; to work rainsing animals, as cattle and horses, working the earth, agriculture, they sowing wheat. Their methods of sowing and reaping however, were extremely primitive. ... Some times they got knifes of metal, cloth and pretty things for a change of the work that they made.

At first glance, this writing might not seem impressive. But I was struck by its authenticity. It contrasted sharply with the copied writing from the first project. From my perspective as an ESL teacher, when beginning ESL students are doing research, the more mistakes the better. This shows me they are finding information, comprehending what it means, and trying to write it in their own words. It shows me that they have thought about the writing. Most ESL students have a hard time with this. Often I receive beautifully-copied yet tedious reports on the assigned topics. In this same report, Elana, one of Marisol's group members, wrote about the religion of the Spanish:

Whatever the Spaniards may have done, good or bad, reflects in the final analysis the fact that from the beginning of their history, they had to face and deal with the most disastrous and unfortunate conditions of the growing of the Mohammedan occupation. Spanish religion ... is a form of belief that is characteristic of Spain, intelligible only within the peculiar causticity of her history.

As I stated previously, it is easy to see when ESL students are copying. After only a few months in the country, it is impossible for them to write error-free. Elana, in fact, was a very bright student. She may very well have understood what she wrote here. But the point is, all she did was locate the information in a book and copy it. She might have made some decisions as to which portions of the information to include, but there was not much else going on here.

In contrast, Marisol's writing had many errors. There were spelling mistakes like "rainsing" (raising), and syntax problems like "they sowing wheat" and "for a change of the work." But what gratified me was that she was working with the language. She was not just reading a book and lifting passages from it. She had found information and was trying to write about what the Spanish cowboys did for their livelihood. It wasn't fantastic writing, but it was authentic. Marisol too was pleased with her final project. In her reflection log she wrote about her group:

> They are very good as partners. They were working hard. We shared ideas each other. How they work and what kind of ideas they have. ... We did the best, that we could do. We getting informations from differents book from the library. We really like this group. We shared opionions about how to do our work. I think we had a good organitation.

Marisol was still struggling in her writing. The spelling in "organitation", and the "s" in "differents" indicate that Marisol is probably still translating from Spanish. But her message is clear. "We did the best, that we could do. We shared opinions about how to do our work." Those are the issues that are important to Marisol.

Several months later, I asked her to tell me what kind of processes her final group used in working together:

> We getting informations from differents book from the library. We all went to the library, and we each got a book. We each read it. I was understanding all the context first. Then I write by myself.

The processes depicted here are quite different from her description of the early projects when she was translating from Spanish. Now Marisol was reading the information first, trying to understand it in English and then trying to write it in her words.

I thought back to Marisol's first reflection when she had been asked if she enjoyed working in groups. "Yes, because you can to compare opinion and to the work better." Two and a half months later she wrote, "We did the best, that we could do. ... We shared opionions about how to do our work. I think we had a good organitation."

It was the exact same sentiment, only this time she had said it much more clearly. I noted with pride the growth in her writing. I asked her which project she had enjoyed the most:

> The mixed group was better. That way we have to speak English. Mixed group. They speak English. ... It's nice cuz we were laughing and everything, you know, enjoying the work. With Claudia, Brenda, (the self-chosen group) everybody agree. We divided the work to every people. Every people was doing the work. In other group, Igor, I make Igor's work, and then I help Min Yong doing the map.

Brenda from Hong Kong and Liana from Armenia were dependable. They were good students and friends. That was more important to Marisol than working with someone who spoke Spanish.

I thought back to her reflection from the first project on North Beach when she had worked with an all Spanish-speaking group. She said she had learned nothing. Now, although her writing still had a way to go, I saw progress in her writing and thinking.

She was working with a heterogeneous group, overcoming language and social barriers and, more importantly, valuing the group process.

A year later I asked Marisol to reflect one final time on what she had learned in the class. She talked about the second project when she had worked in a mixed-language group: "I like sharing opinions. He's (Igor) giving me opinions and ideas. Maybe his opinion is better than mine. It's good to get ideas." When asked if she liked working with partners, she replied, "Yes. Because four heads think better than one."

Marisol was clearly able to see the power of working and learning from other students. Perhaps she was echoing what the Russian psychologist Vygotsky called the "zone of proximal development," the importance of students learning with and from each other.

Findings
By listening to Marisol and my other students, I have developed insights into four important aspects of instruction in my classroom.

1. Language and Group Work
From studying the transcript of Marisol's mixed group and looking at her reflections, I learned that the group work had value. It was, as I thought, providing opportunities for students to have authentic conversations and to practice their new language.

Marisol's mixed-language group provided lots of cognitive language proficiency. There was discussion of academic issues. As stated, this is an area in which many ESL students are weak. In studying a transcript of a group meeting, I saw a complex discussion going on between Marisol and Igor on the use of paragraphs and the third person singular. Marisol and Igor were learning from each other. Though the two other students in the group, Alejandro and Min Yong, were not able to take part in the discussion because of their lower English skills, Marisol and Igor were able to talk about important issues. They were getting lots of CALP and, although it may not have been pleasurable or fun, Marisol's discussions and negotiations with Igor were valuable opportunities for both of them to use English in difficult but meaningful ways. I suspect ESL students do not have many opportunities to have such content-based discussions in English.

2. Copying

Copying is not a simple issue. While it inevitably comes up every semester, before this research I had not really had an opportunity to reflect on what is involved in copying. What may look like direct copying to the teacher may involve several processes by the student. Marisol taught me to look beyond what was written on the paper. Early in the semester I had accused her of copying some sentences from a pamphlet. Marisol was indignant at the accusation. While she admitted that she had lifted some of the writing, she was miffed that I had not validated the other parts of her writing which she had worked hard on. By talking to her, I was able to get a deeper understanding of the group process and of why she had resorted to copying. By only mentioning the copying and not validating the other parts of her writing, I had erred.

However, I have developed strong beliefs about copying. I believe that especially for ESL students, the number of errors can indicate growth in writing. In doing research, copying is a problem for most ESL students. I suspect it is a problem for native speakers also. But beginning ESL students have a great deal of trouble doing research in English. Invariably, they tend to copy large segments of information from books. I go to great lengths to explain to them that I want their own words, even if there are mistakes. One former student once went home to her parent and complained, "I don't understand. My teacher wants me to make mistakes." Yes, I do. If I see mistakes, I see that the student is working with the language, trying to adapt it to his or her own words. Liana's report on California was smooth and effortless. Even though she may have understood what she wrote, she just copied it from a book. Marisol's writing in the same report was not as smooth. There were many errors. But these errors showed me that she was reading the information in the book, comprehending it, and then trying to write it in her own words. That process of taking the information in, thinking about it, and then trying to write in her own words is, I believe, intrinsically valuable.

3. Grouping

I looked at Marisol in three kinds of groups over the semester: an all-Spanish speaking group, a mixed-language group, and a group self-chosen by Marisol. She surprised me when she said it didn't make any difference to her, whether her group was heterogeneously-mixed or grouped by language. I thought she would appreciate the luxury of communicating in Spanish with her group members. But Marisol taught me that there were other factors to consider. What mattered most to Marisol was how hard each group member worked.

Toward the end of the semester when Marisol was given the choice to work with whomever she wanted, she chose to work with an Armenian, a Chinese, and an El Salvadoran girl. The fact that they were good friends was very important, but equally important was, as Marisol stated, that they were all good workers. It was important to Marisol not only to have fun, but also to work hard. When I asked her how they communicated, she whimsically replied, "No. Not is problem because we … we can speak with … with the hands!"

I must be very careful in extrapolating my findings about Marisol for all ESL students. I must emphasize that Marisol came into my class with a lot of advantages over other students. She came from a literate home environment. She had strong literacy skills in her own language. There was a native English speaker living in her household. She had confidence. She had distinct advantages over many other students.

While for Marisol a bilingual group was not so important, I do not wish this study to show that bilingual groups or studying is not effective. I am a strong believer in bilingual education. I believe that students who do not have the same academic background as Marisol need the primary language assistance much more. Marisol's academic background prepared her to lean less and less on her primary language. Her level of English proficiency was intermediate. Studies have shown that at this level, students can receive more and more instruction in their second language.

4. Students as Communicators

Marisol's strongest suit was that she was a communicator. She had very little of what Krashen calls the "affective filter," the shyness or inhibition that stops many people from attempting to speak in a second language. When she spoke or wrote, she concentrated on getting her point across. She did not worry about form. In the conversation with Igor, we see her using an array of strategies to get her point across, gesturing, repeating, and intoning so that Igor will understand how to use paragraphs. Many ESL students do not have this same confidence. They fear that they will make a mistake or be laughed at. They worry so much about being grammatically correct, or about how they sound, that they forget about communicating. They play it safe. Marisol, however, felt no compunction at venturing out into the deep water, expressing her feelings, even her anger at the teacher when I questioned the authenticity of her writing.

When she was asked a question, she would almost always attempt to give an answer. If not understood, she would work at responding in a different way. Her English was not perfect, but she didn't care. She wanted to get her point across. Most beginning ESL students do not share this same level of confidence. They might attempt to give a one-word answer or short phrase, but if they make a mistake, or they are not understood, they are often stymied and do not go any further. Perhaps if we can get other students to lower their affective filter and display some of that confidence that Marisol displayed, their progress in acquiring English will be enhanced.

Conclusion

Marisol has since departed to another high school, and now I find myself asking what a colleague of mine from Boston once asked about teacher research: "So what?"

First off, I learned a lot about my classroom. I got an opportunity to get an up close view of the group projects I have been orchestrating over the last ten years. For the first time I looked closely at some groups, observing what was going on. As teachers, we are constantly making assumptions and judgments about what we see everyday. Through this inquiry I was able to check out some of my assumptions.

From this research I also learned the value of getting multiple perspectives of the classroom. The teacher's view of the classroom, while valuable, is just one piece of the puzzle. By adding the students', visitors' and even other teachers' perspectives, a much richer view of the classroom emerges.

A teacher's day is so jam-packed with responsibilities above and beyond the teaching that there is little time for reflection. In between teaching, parent conferences, writing interim reports, and running to the Xerox machine, we rarely have time to breathe during the day. By setting aside time each day to sit and reflect, I received a much deeper picture of the classroom than the spontaneous snapshots I take in my mind every day. I would urge other teachers to begin keeping journals or begin writing about their classrooms. I would encourage them to see if there are other teachers at their school or in their area who are interested in forming a "teacher research" group. The camaraderie and support from my group was most welcome.

Listening to Marisol gave me an opportunity to look closely at a student beyond the cursory glances of writing samples and tests. Through her writing, her talking, her actions, and her reflecting, Marisol helped me to see that there was real work and talk going on in the groups. But watching and listening to Marisol always seemed to turn back on me, the teacher. By looking at Marisol I was able to look in the mirror — not my mirror, but a student's mirror — and see how her perceptions supported or differed from mine.

Perhaps in some ways what I found out about Marisol was not so important. What remains for me is the process, the experience of looking at my class from different perspectives and, more importantly, the benefits from listening to my students.

A version of this article has appeared in the Fall 1995 CATESOL Journal.

Looking at Classrooms

Looking at Classrooms

Urban teachers share a common and not very comforting knowledge: In diverse and multicultural classrooms there is no guarantee that the old ways are the best ways. Hence, in cities, committed and energetic teachers look for new ways to win permanent converts to the pleasures of learning. While Bob Fecho, Carole Miller and Christine Cziko teach in varied situations and take different approaches, all are asking the question, "What can I do to nudge my students to become more capable, involved and enthusiastic learners?"

Learning from Laura

by

Bob Fecho

T MIGHT have been an insignificant exchange. Marsha, who teaches next to me, had returned a draft of teacher research I had conducted in which I had investigated my students' perceptions of language and power. As an Eastern-European American English teacher of primarily working class African Americans, I have been concerned about the ways language can be used to exclude students from full participation in mainstream culture. Specifically, if my students are adept at reading, discussing, and composing texts in ways which showcase their abilities to handle complex material, why are these strengths frequently ignored by mainstream employers and admissions officers if the students use dialect to write about and discuss these texts?

Further, I have been curious about whether these students view language as a means of gaining political and social power for themselves and their community. In other words, what were my students' attitudes about acquiring standard English? Did they connect standard English with some sort of mainstream power access? Was their struggle with consistent use of standard English a question of an inability to code switch — something I never believed — or was it more a case of a lack of desire, need, or inclination to accept the privileged dialect? And, perhaps, was it even a form of either conscious or subconscious resistance? As a result of these interests, I had begun collecting data about the ways my students perceived, discussed and used language.

There in the hallway between classes Marsha said, "I can see why you hated to lose to Laura. Laura, for you, was like Jeremy and Malisha for me. Laura pushed your thinking. She challenged you. Her thoughts were complex and not easy."

I mumbled some agreeing response and thanked Marsha for this and her other comments. That might have been that — just two urban teachers chatting shop between bells. But Marsha's words stayed with me: "Laura pushed your own thinking." Marsha's words made sense, but how had Laura pushed and challenged my ideas?

Laura had been a student in my English class — a new admit who was designated to be in her junior year, but was hoping to amass enough credits to graduate. For a student new to the school, she was more outgoing than most and almost immediately carved a niche for herself in the social structure of the program. She had the unique ability both to be widely accepted by her peers and to be widely appreciated for her academics by the teaching staff. Always energetic, she had an ability to spark lively discussion because she cared about ideas and enjoyed being challenged by counterarguments. It was during these moments that her insight would emerge full-blown in the classroom, laid out for the taking.

Triggered by Marsha's words, I mentally scanned the legacy Laura had left from her year in my classroom — her writings, her class responses, our private conversations. I realized that often during this time I had been the learner and Laura had been the teacher. How had Laura affected the way I saw my role as a teacher of English, the occupation which Gee (1987, p. 743) characterizes as "at the heart of the most crucial educational, cultural and political issues of our time"?

In this article I want to share ways that Laura believes language affects her life. I also want to document the dialogue I have had with Laura as a way of illustrating how this dialogue changed me and changed the teaching and learning in our classroom. Particularly, I want to show how Laura caused me to modify the beliefs I had acquired from language theoreticians as I examined how these views connected or failed to connect to the lives of my students. To make these points, I have drawn on excerpts from class transcripts, an interview with Laura, her language-focused autobiography, and her own research into language.

Why My Classroom Suited Laura

I have always believed that students, when fully engaged in the classroom, make teachers reassess their beliefs and ways of teaching. My classroom — like other classrooms in the school-within-a school at which I teach — is structured for student involvement. If it weren't firmly lodged in a secondary school, my class might be considered a whole language classroom. In this environment heterogeneously grouped students, read, write, talk and reflect by themselves, in pairs, as small groups and as an entire class. We use texts to generate more texts. For example, this year students read *Oedi-*

pus and then, as one option, wrote updated, urbanized versions of this classic tale. For example, one group of students set the play as a war for drug territory with Oedipus as an undercover cop, while another group moved the play into corporate head-quarters where Oedipus became the CEO. Not limited to or by the canon, students delved into Toni Morrison and Zora Neale Hurston, in part to explore issues of power and gender such as what it means to be a woman and an African American in a society which has a history of devaluing both attributes. I tried to structure nontraditional assignments. Rather than answering questions after reading a story, students connected literature and the world around them in ways that moved from the personal to the academic as when students used journal responses to generate more formal essays. Then as now in my classroom, I have tried to establish an atmosphere in which students value learning, connect it to their lives and view it as a means of gaining power beyond their communities.

How Theory Has Affected My Teaching

I have been influenced by the theories of critical and multicultural pedagogy. Of the former, the work of Paulo Friere, Ira Shor, and Henry Giroux continue to force me to research and analyze my own practice to seek better ways to engage my students with questions which help them to make meaning of their own worlds. To this end, the class is structured with an essential question (Sizer 1984) which acts as a lens for the entire year and unifies the ongoing work of the classroom. When Laura was my student, the question was, "How does learning connect you to your world?" We were then able to particularize that to "How does learning about language connect you to your world?" This question then provided a framework with which we were able to investigate not only the structure of language, but the effect it has on our lives. Regarding multicultural pedagogy, the work of Lisa Delpit, Shirley Brice Heath, and John Ogbu are stimuli for ongoing review of the ways I teach, as Delpit has put it, "other people's children." Specifically, the year-long study of language was prompted by Heath's belief in student-based ethnographic research, Ogbu's concern about what qualifies as caste minority resistance, and Delpit's insistence that minority students must be appreciated for their home dialects while being given access to the power dialect. The result was a year in which language took center stage, not as a mass of rules to be memorized and accepted but as a subject for inquiry and options.

How Laura Brought Me Down to Earth

I saw the language-power relationship as leading to mainstream culture. It was Laura who made me see that language was also, most immediately, a way to power on the street. She wrote about a friend:

> *Some people use profanity because they feel powerful. ... And my one girlfriend ... she use profanity because she put effort into it, she put stress into it because people are scared of her when she talk like that. She don't get in too many fights by her mouth, she can talk her way out of it, or talk her way into a fight, or talk somebody out of wanting to fight her, because of the way she speaks. She uses a lot of profanity and slang and that'll make a person think that she's from the streets and knows how to fight, so you really wouldn't want to mess with her.*

While some part of me already knew what Laura was saying, I had fallen so deeply into my reading about the politics of language that I had forgotten how important peer relationships were among adolescents. I saw facility with language as a way for individuals and groups to access the mainstream power structures. Laura reminded me that for most adolescents perceptions of power begin at a more basic level — among peers. When my students reflect on issues of power, they see power first of all in the context of an adolescent hierarchy. To them, the tough who will seemingly say anything to anybody, the girl who knows the latest slang before anyone else, and the guy who can recite raps as well as the CD all hold some power or sway in the lunchrooms and locker-rooms of the school, if not in the academic classroom. This culture of the corridors is of primary importance to the students. Acceptance among one's peers is more necessary than acceptance by the teachers, so more attention — conscious and subconscious — is paid to acquisition of slang than to gaining standard English.

If students can't at the onset relate the connection between language and power to their immediate circumstances, it is useless to expect them to extrapolate to some abstract future need or mainstream cultural expectation.

Laura's mere presence served as an example of the way language could be a source of power both on the street and in the mainstream culture, in the school hallways and in the school classroom. I believe it was her facility in both cultures which made her a leader in the class. As a spokesperson for the group, particularly early in the year, Laura was often the first to voice an idea before the rest of the class felt comfortable enough to risk their own responses. Hearing what Laura had to say, others would nod assent, testify to the credibility of her view or offer their own anecdotes.

How Laura Made Prominent the Dilemma of Dialects

While Laura reminded me that language meant power on the streets, she also understood that language brought or blocked the access to the mainstream, depending upon one's facility with the mainstream dialect. Her comments brought into focus the inner conflict that results when language forces someone to choose between the language of the home, and the language of the existing power culture. Like many of my students, Laura was able to slide among three dialects — home, street, and academic. What singled out Laura from her peers was that she was much more in command of all three and more clear about the situations which dictated use of each. Therefore, her language was usually one of choice rather than one of accommodation. Coming from a home where she often meets, in her words, "people of higher intellect and lifestyles" and is encouraged to read books and watch PBS, Laura has made a conscious decision not to fall into patterns of slang and profanity:

> *As time went on, I found myself not liking to speak this street slang any longer. I felt as though I could accomplish more with an intelligent background and I must say that I have accomplished more.*

She acknowledges that at one time speaking street slang and profanity had advantages in her peer group:

> *So if I had a friend who used profanity because he or she felt powerful by using it and I wanted to hang out with that person, I myself wouldn't use profanity. But that's why a lot of [other students] use it. Like most of the people I interviewed, they didn't get it from their home environment. They got it from school. And in the streets. That's how.*

But now she states, "My knowledge (of standard English) helps me in life whereas their ignorance hurts them."

Laura knew her language systems were in conflict. She was equally facile moving from standard to slang and on into variations of both. Writing about this ability, she mentioned the following:

> *As a child, I also spoke [slang]. Being part of more than one environment, I had to adjust myself. I had to know when and*

> *where was the time to speak this way. I was brought up to speaking proper English, and to hear me speak [in slang] was sort of a shock. … Mother always thought that if I spoke [slang] continuously, I would soon adapt to this way of speaking. She knew that this was how the children were talking, but the only difference was her child was not allowed to talk like this. I didn't associate with many people, but at times when I did, I wanted to be in, be a part of the crowd. This was how and why I began to speak like the other children.*

It is evident that the language expectations of Laura's peers differed from those of her mother, and she found herself — as she wrote elsewhere — having to shift between dialect which would "keep respect for myself and also for my mother," and dialect which would allow her — as noted above — to mesh with peers. It is interesting to note that Laura seems more concerned about using language in a manner that her mother or her peers might approve than in trying to meet the standard of some faceless mainstream culture. Less immediate and more abstract, that mainstream culture holds only secondary status in motivating her decisions about language choice.

How Laura Conducted Research on Language

All students in my class were expected to carry out an inquiry project investigating some question regarding language which had come up over the course of a year. Completed over two months time and requiring the students to conduct interviews and observational research, the studies gave the students opportunities to decide on some personal inquiry into language and to then seek data which would help them to better understand their question and, as a next step, to make that learning evident to the rest of the class. Laura, to no one's surprise, chose to examine why students elect to use profanity and slang and the effect it has on their lives. Among other things, she noticed that her peers showed equal proficiency at deciding "...where to speak [profanity] and where not to speak it." Furthermore, Laura concluded that "this foul language was up from the streets and from friends. Not one of my interviews said that they learned it from home environment." She went on to explain that

> ...language is formed from the society in which you live. I think children who hear slang speak it because it's natural and it's not taught to them as being wrong. ...You pick up things that aren't necessarily good or bad, but because you see it and hear it, it becomes a part of you.

The issues we raised about language led Laura to this point of research and this set of conclusions which, as she was able to verbalize, "only raises many more questions about language." While acknowledging that peers code switch, Laura differs from many of her peers, however, in that she has more opportunity, through family and social connections, to practice these code switches. Additionally, she seems more cognizant of the opportunities these switches present and of their importance in her life. By understanding this about Laura, I was able to get a better sense of those students who struggled more as they attempted to cross these language borders. What seemed evident from Laura was that family support and a conscious choice on her part were able to propel her into choosing to use standard English if the situation called for it. For most of my students, however, that family support was less obvious and could be contradictory, so election of standard English and continued practice outside of school would be less forthcoming.

How Laura Caused Me to Re-think "Black English"
Perhaps the most significant way that Laura pushed my thinking centered around the concepts of Black English and standard English. From the research I knew that the term "Black

English" was conceived to designate a distinct dialect with a regular grammar specific primarily to African American speakers (Dillard, 1972; Labov, 1972). The commonly accepted intent of the research was to lend legitimacy to the dialect and to dispel beliefs that the dialect was nothing more than random errors against standard English. I also knew that the use of the term and the dialect was celebrated by many African American educators (Jordan, 1988; Smitherman, 1977) and that the dialect figured prominently in the works of such celebrated African American writers as Zora Neale Hurston, Alice Walker, and August Wilson. As I introduced the concept to my classes, I did so fully expecting they would embrace the term and the concept behind it.

I was wrong. In fact, many students objected. And Laura was among the first and was perhaps the most passionate in her questioning. Most protests revolved around the idea that no matter how much one tried to celebrate Black English as a vibrant dialect, the fact that it wasn't standard English condemned it to be viewed as nonstandard English and inferior by inference. As Laura pointed out in an interview:

> *Well first, my objection was why label Black English Black English. I mean, people speak slang all over. Now they say they have standard English and nonstandard English. There's slang. Why label something — OK, there's slang or nonstandard English that a white person might speak. It's not labeled white English. It's just called, nonstandard English. Why, and then it seems our world consists of so many racial problems as there is, I don't understand why would they label a black person speaking nonstandard English, why put a label on it? Why couldn't it just be called nonstandard English, or incorrect use of language.*

Even in this flat transcript, one can almost hear the urgency and concern in her voice as she argues to remove the racial identity from the label and thus eliminate one more inference of supposed inferiority.

It's not that Laura didn't see the strength and vibrancy of what is commonly construed as Black English. During discussions of Ntozake Shange's *For Colored Girls Who Have Considered Suicide/When the Rainbow is Enuf,* she recognized how the language of the streets made the work come alive. In a class discussion where several students questioned the appropriateness of the author's use of Black English and slang, she said, "People speak like that. It's nothing wrong with it." However, Laura felt that any term connecting African Americans to what she viewed as one more so-called separate-but-equal ranking was unacceptable. And she told me so in speech and in writing:

> *Labels. Why labels are put into it. Now, like the researchers on the Oprah Winfrey show. They have objections. Some are for black people learning how to speak standard language, but it'll never be clear. Just like racism will never be completely gone, it'll never be clear. It'll just be hidden, or covered or just pushed to the side. But it'll never be clear.*

For Laura there is nothing to be gained through the use of Black English as a label because the term neither takes in the range of dialects spoken by African Americans nor gives them credit for speaking anything but non-accepted dialect.

For myself the objections of Laura and others forced me to reconsider my assumptions. If nothing else, I realized I had to give the opinions of my students the same weight I assigned to Labov and Smitherman. While I could present to students arguments for celebrating Black English, I also had to accept their resistance to the concept. The questions that Laura and others raised, while lacking academic pedigree, were nonetheless valid and needed equal consideration on my part. While I could enter these discussions with my own beliefs, I had to realize that those beliefs must be as open to change as those of my students. If the classroom was to be a place where opinions were engaged, then individuals needed to be able to make choices to adopt or adapt. If I wanted my students to raise issues, I had to take these issues seriously, consider them, and allow them to stand or fall on their merit.

Perhaps more surprisingly, Laura's thoughts led me to re-think the very concept of Black English and its relationship to standard English. Black English had been a relatively new and thus less steady construct in my thinking than standard English, but now even my considerations of standard English became wobbly. I began to challenge my beliefs that had been at the very core of my life first as an English learner and then as an English teacher. I began to see how labels like Black English and standard English were loaded and were either restrictive or privileging. As we have noted, the mere act of calling one dialect "standard" relegates all other dialects to substandard or, at least, unprivileged. From another tack, how do we account for a range of dialects in the Black community under one label, "Black English"? This insight sent me hunting for terms to use in their stead. "Home language," "peer language" and "mainstream language," although not without some baggage, seemed more personal and accepting because they credit the influences that affect our language choices. On the other hand, I realize that by denying the direct influence of race, we may lose an opportunity to celebrate a language worthy of pride. On this subject I am torn.

How Laura Changed Me
Which brings us to the last of Laura's legacies. Our talks around language left me more conflicted than I was before they began.

But conflict, perhaps, is not so terrible. In fact, I believe that's what I was seeking. Classrooms can be seen as endpoints (we have arrived) or resting points (we are moving in a direction). Teachers can be conveyers of truth or seekers of truer paths. I prefer the latter. To me, the year is divided into countless learning events, each one moving students and teachers closer to goals they never reach but can only approach. As Laura noted, inquiry into slang led to a greater understanding of slang on her part, but also to more questions for future inquiry. What she thought was a termination — knowing more about slang — was only a dot on an infinite continuum of learning about language. By opening up my classroom to discussions about language issues which touched the lives of Laura and her peers, I shook my assumptions, challenged my beliefs, and stirred my curiosity. My transactions with Laura reminded me that no matter how trite, the lyric "if you become a teacher, by your pupils you'll be taught" is consummately true and critical for an inquiry-based classroom.

As a teacher helping students cope with the complexities of the coming century, I seek to help them feel comfortable in uncertainty.

Although Laura's work in my class left me in conflict, it was not the kind of conflict that immobilizes and prevents growth. Even today, three years after these discussions, those conflicts and ideas energize my classroom. As a daily practice, I work at having all students consider the import of language in all texts, particularly the texts they create for themselves. Language is still seen as a topic for continuing inquiry, and students are encouraged to raise questions about the impact of such language in their lives. What we have realized together is that issues of language are too critical to be ignored and too important to be left solely to the experts.

References

Delpit, L. (1988). The silenced dialogue: Power and pedagogy in educating other people's children. *Harvard Education Review, 58,* 280-298.

Dillard, J. (1972). *Black English, its history and usage in the United States.* New York: Vintage.

Freire, P. (1970). *Pedagogy of the oppressed.* New York: Continuum.

Gee, J. (1987). Orality and literacy: From the savage mind to ways with words. *TESOL Quarterly, 20,* 719-746.

Giroux, H. (1985) Intellectual label and pedagogical work: Rethinking the role of teachers as intellectuals. *Phenomenology and Pedagogy, 3,* 20-31.

Heath, S. B. (1983). *Ways with words: Language, life and work in communities and classrooms.* New York: Cambridge University Press.

Jordan, J. (1988). Nobody mean more to me than you and the future life of Willie Jordan. *Harvard Educational Review, 58,* 363-374.

Labov, W. (1972). *Language in the inner city: Studies in the black English vernacular.* Oxford: Basil Blackwell.

Ogbu, J. (1987). Opportunity structure, cultural boundaries and literacy. In J. Langer (Ed.) *Language, literature, and culture: Issues of society and schooling.* Norwood, NJ: Ablex.

Shor, I. (1980). *Critical teaching & everyday life.* Chicago: The University of Chicago Press.

Sizer, T. (1984). *Horace's compromise.* Boston: Houghton Mifflin.

Smitherman, G. (1977). *Talkin' and testifyin': The language of black America.* Boston: Houghton Mifflin.

No Longer "Too White":

Using Multicultural Literature to Promote Academic Achievement and Cultural Understanding

by
CAROLE MILLER

E BEGAN the first day of school sitting in a circle and introducing ourselves in English and Spanish. Looking at my twenty-seven new third graders, I was thinking of Chantelle, an African American girl who had now gone on to fourth grade. I remembered how she had told me that she had been afraid to speak Spanish on the first day of school last year for fear that she would "turn into a Spanish person." Now I was trying to make my new students comfortable, modeling phrases and having the group say them together before asking each child to use them individually.

We were beginning the second year of an experimental program which gave me a class composed of equal numbers of bilingual program students and regular education students. Our school was large and urban, with a diverse student population: 62% Latino, 26% African American, and 12% European American. At each grade level, there were two or three regular education classes and two Spanish bilingual classes whose students were integrated minimally with regular education students. I taught one of those bilingual classes for 17 years before reaching out to regular education colleagues to escape the isolation which weighed on me personally and which, I believed, was depriving my students of models and incentives for speaking, reading and writing English. For a few years, two regular education teachers and I integrated our students during the language arts period. Finally, we decided to make the big jump to total integration. We sent letters to the parents of all second grade students, outlining the integrated, language-rich, experiential program we envisioned.

From the pool of bilingual and regular education students who opted for our program, we created three classes. A third of each class was drawn from the bilingual program. For the first time most of my students were African American or European American.

The first year of the experiment brought the expected challenges, joys and frustrations. But teaching African American students for the first time also brought something completely unforeseen and initially most unwelcome: the gradual realization that race was an unresolved issue for me. I explored my reactions to students' comments and classroom incidents during that first year as part of the Urban Sites Writing Network, a coalition of teachers doing research in their classrooms, and I delved deep into my background for answers. I learned that my characteristic response to whatever makes me feel uncomfortable is to put on blinders or "sweep it under the rug." I also learned that living in another country, acquiring a second language and teaching Latino children for many years had not enabled me to move beyond my own culture. I ruefully faced the fact that I was very much the product of the white suburbs of the 1950s and that my cultural identity influenced every aspect of my teaching, including the curriculum I had so proudly created.

Now beginning the second year and armed with new self-understandings, I would be working with only one regular education teacher, Judy Weisenberger. Half my students would be drawn from the regular education program and half from the bilingual program. Because I spoke Spanish and Judy didn't, I kept those students who were completely monolingual in Spanish. We also agreed that the bilingual paraprofessional would spend most of her time in Judy's class.

—— • ——

I looked around the circle. There was much that I did not yet know about the twenty-seven students sitting with me. Two of my six African American students would move within a few weeks. Of the four who remained, one was Elaine — moody, talkative and brilliant. Irene, also African American, had been Elaine's best friend in second grade. Irene was a good student, too, and most anxious to learn Spanish. Kamal, quiet and small, was the only African American boy. The fourth African American student was Tanya, who smiled a lot but never let me get to know her. In an attempt to understand her sometimes passive-aggressive behavior, I made an appointment with her mother. After four broken appointments, an aunt finally appeared who could cast no light on the problem.

The five European American students included Peter, whose mother had a responsible position at a local university and who was one of a relatively small number of parents who were active in school affairs. Jennifer, blonde and blue-eyed, had also been coded "white" by her Cuban mother and European American father. She understood spoken Spanish but hesitated to use it and did not read it. Joe's grandparents had been born in Ireland; he was an only child living with his mother and grandparents. Katie, too, was of Irish descent; she was tough and pugnacious, often feuding with Joe. Of the seventeen students coded "Latino," thirteen were enrolled in the bilingual program. Seven of these students spoke little English, and only two of them read fairly well in Spanish. One of these students, Cesar, was a gifted artist. He was thin, bespectacled and possessed of an extraordinary imagination. Eva and Julia, also enrolled in the bilingual program, were of Puerto Rican and Costa Rican parents respectively. Both were excellent students, articulate and interested. Wilfredo was a dark-skinned Honduran with good Spanish skills and a mercurial temper. Marta was the baby of her family and the apple of her father's eye. I had to gently dissuade him from accompanying his daughter to the classroom door each morning. The Latino students who were enrolled in the regular education program included Hector, an extremely intelligent but troubled student, whose parents were both HIV positive; and Gisela, one of the best English readers in the class who, along with Elaine, would be selected for the Advanced Work class for fourth grade.

"Me llamo…" I repeated for Kamal, leaning forward encouragingly. "Me llamo Kamal" he answered, somewhat uncomfortably. Alejandro flashed a big grin but remained mute as I repeated several times, "My name is Alejandro." Finally, after breaking the phrases down into separate words, I got him to repeat each one. "Good, Alejandro," I said, ignoring the suppressed but not unfriendly giggles of his new classmates.

I told them that I wanted each of them to write a goal for themselves. My own goal, I confided, was to listen to them and learn from them. I also asked them to write about themselves, and modeled what I had in mind by reading what I had written about myself. "My first name is Carole," I read. "I'm 49 years old, I've been married for nine years, and I've been a teacher for 20 years. On the day after Christmas, I'll be turning 50! To celebrate, my husband and I will be going to Hawaii for two weeks. Do you have any questions?"

"Do you have any children?" Eva asked politely.

"No," I said.

"Just us," murmured Gisela.

"Did you go to college to become a teacher, Mrs. Miller?" Elaine asked. I answered all their questions. I wanted from the beginning to present myself as a real person. Facades and blinders seemed to go together and were, I had discovered during the previous year, counterproductive. How could I grapple with searingly real issues like racism from behind a facade? I felt comfortable acknowledging the details of my life which diverged the most from parallel details in their lives — my age, for instance. Yes, I was much, much older than they were, a fact which had advantages as well as disadvantages. We would look at things differently because of that, and both points of view had their uses. It was good for me to reflect once again that my cultural reality was one but not the only reality — nor, necessarily, the best reality.

I had two goals for my students. First, I wanted them to connect with the curriculum culturally, racially and linguistically. Before students can learn, they must be able to relate to what is taught. Second, I wanted them to move beyond their culturally-shaped points of view, to entertain new perspectives. If they (and I) are to interact productively with others in a diverse society, we need to appreciate that people view reality from a variety of perspectives and that opening oneself to someone else's point of view can be an enlightening, enriching experience.

My pursuit of these goals began as I set up my classroom for that first day. I displayed two poems, chosen because their themes were similar and appropriate.

One was "Neighborhood Street" from *Night on Neighborhood Street* by Eloise Greenfield, and the other was "Buenos Vecinos" (Good Neighbors) by Alma Flor Ada. Between the poems I put enlarged color photocopies and illustrations from the Greenfield book showing children of color jumping rope and talking together. I displayed around the room new multicultural hard cover books and books in Spanish which I had purchased during the previous spring and summer.

The sheer quantity of trade books (which prompted one disoriented visitor to pause on the threshold and remark, "This must be the library") testified to the important role literature would play in my curriculum. The ever-increasing multicultural orientation of the collection suggested the kind of curriculum I wished to create. In the course of the school year, multicultural literature would not only shape our reading program but would generate and support our class discussions, our writing, our social studies, art, music and even some of our math activities.

Independent Reading Connects Students to Their Cultures

There were many opportunities to read independently. We began each afternoon with twenty minutes of silent, independent reading; but, at other times, whenever students finished their work early, they were encouraged to "choose a book." I paid careful attention to the books they were choosing. I noticed that African American children were selecting books about African Americans, so I went through the classroom library and put more books about African Americans on display. But it wasn't only the African American children who looked for books about themselves. I couldn't help smiling when Rosa, on her first day of school in the United States, literally skipped back to her seat with a book which to her joy and incredulity was written in Spanish.

Students sometimes connected with books which were not specifically part of their culture but had special meaning for them. This was the case when Kamal read *Rainbow Crow*. It is a Native American legend of how the crow came to be black, with glossy black feathers in which all the other colors are reflected. Kamal, my only male African American student, lingered over that book, choosing it over and over.

Students Make Connections Between Cultures

Multicultural literature afforded us the opportunity to make intriguing connections between cultures. When we studied spiders, I read aloud *Anansi the Spider* by Gerald McDermott. Many students were familiar with this tale, drawn from West African folklore, about a clever spider and his sons. The book I read the following day, though, was new. *Anancy and Mr. Dry Bone* by Fiona French was set in the Caribbean. Anancy, though a man and not a spider, was clever and outwitted Mr. Dry Bone to "get the girl." We compared the stories and talked about how traditions move with people from place to place and are adapted to new surroundings.

Corn was a topic with ties to many cultures. I read aloud *Dragonfly's Tale,* a Zuni story about a people who are allowed to experience famine by the Corn Maidens as punishment for wasting corn. The kindness of two children and the intervention of a dragonfly fashioned from a cornstalk restore the village. My partner Judy found "Why Corn Has Silky White Hair," a Southern tale about an old man who persuades Death that he is too busy tending his corn crop to go with him. Mindful from years spent in Guatemala how important corn was to the Mayas and their descendants, I put up a poster of the Mayan corn god, Yum Kax, and read aloud *Song of the Chirimia,* a Guatemalan tale. "What story does this remind you of?" I asked the class when I finished. "It's a lot like *Anancy and Mr. Dry Bone,"* Elaine volunteered, and pointed out the structural similarities. "Yes," I agreed. "Isn't it interesting how different groups of people tell the same story in such different ways?"

With all this talk about corn, I decided to have students make corn tortillas. It was a decision I wouldn't have made a year earlier, probably because it was not part of the cultural traditions of any of my students. Now it made sense to me, as part of my other goal, "to help students acquire a new perspective." I brought the moistened corn meal from student to student so they could smell it. Then I showed them how to make a ball and flatten it, smoothing the edges, and then how to pat it thin, passing it from one hand to the other. While we patted, we chanted in Spanish an adaptation of a traditional rhyme about tortillas:

> *Tortillitas, tortillitas, tortililitas para mama; tortillitas, tortillitas, tortillitas para papa. (Little tortillas, little tortillas, little tortillas for mother; little tortillas, little tortillas, little tortillas for father).*

The bilingual paraprofessional had brought in the circular piece of metal she used at home to toast tortillas, and we toasted the children's tortillas on the classroom stove.

After making tortillas, Alejandro wrote a story about the corn that grows around his grandmother's house in the rural Dominican Republic. I discovered his story on one of my routine trips around the room, when I pulled up a chair and asked him if he would read me what he was writing. Like everything else he had written, it was unpunctuated, with no spaces between words. But whereas his other writing tended to describe a trip to Chuck E. Cheese or the neighborhood park, this piece was different; this piece cut to the heart of who he was. Though I had never been to the Dominican Republic, this story evoked memories for me of rural Guatemala. I felt excited, partly because of the authenticity of the piece and partly because I sensed I was making contact for the first time with the real Alejandro, for whom the reality he had described was obviously much more meaningful than anything the United States had yet offered him.

Responding to my enthusiasm, the usually shy and reserved child became excited himself and began to relate in Spanish — at what seemed to me to be a speed of a million words a minute — how they roasted the corn and ate it. "Will you share your story with the group?" I begged, remembering that he usually did not answer when called on, having twice refused to go to the board. To my surprise, he said he would. We ushered him, flushed and smiling, to the "author's pillow" and the class gathered around, sitting cross-legged in a circle on the rug. As he read each sentence, it was competently translated by one of his peers. The class asked him many questions, which he answered in a strong, confident voice. Even when the questions began to repeat themselves, he didn't seem to mind, or even to notice! I took the opportunity to remind the other students that they, too, had wonderful stories to share.

The connection of *Cornrows* by Camille Yarbrough to our study of corn was tenuous but irresistible since Irene, one of my African American students, had come to school with her hair beautifully arranged in cornrows. Just as I had been anxious to celebrate the rural Dominican roots of Alejandro, I wanted to acknowledge now what was culturally special and different about Irene. I had come to believe that it isn't differences that divide, but our attitudes about those differences. If I, as a teacher, acknowledge and celebrate differences, it is likely that my students will, too. Racist remarks, which usually reflect a negative attitude toward differences, become untenable in a setting where differences are celebrated.

I gathered the students around me, showed them the cover, and read the title. Glancing at Irene who, unlike Alejandro, usually exuded confidence and loved the limelight, I said, "Irene is going to be the star of the show today. Come up here, so we can see your beautiful cornrows, Irene." Suddenly and uncharacteristically shy, she blushed and squirmed and covered her face, peeking out at us from between her fingers. I began to tell the group about cornrows, then realized that Irene, unable to resist, was imparting whispered spurts of information about her cornrows to those around her. "I have 56 braids!" she whispered. Then, "My aunt did my hair!" Her friend Elaine was not shy at all, pointing out that she had one braid as did Puerto Rican Marta. In the days and weeks that followed, a number of the African American and Latina girls came to school with cornrows and basked in the admiration of their classmates.

Food Continues to Serve as a Link Between Cultures
Corn was not the only food that helped students explore their cultures and connect to others. We read *Yagua Days* about a child of Puerto Rican descent who visits the island for the first time. The book contains a number of Spanish words and phrases and mentions many tropical fruits and vegetables. Hector was especially excited about this book and told us that reading *Yagua Days* was making him hungry!

I brought in a number of the fruits and vegetables. When I mentioned seeing cartons of *quenepas* (a small, round green fruit) at the airport on one of my trips to Puerto Rico, headed (I assumed) to relatives in New York, the Latino students reacted with nods and smiles.

Throughout the school year, families prepared many of the dishes mentioned in *Yagua Days*, like *flan* (custard) and *arroz con potato* (rice with chicken). We consumed these with relish at parties and during oral presentations about students' "roots." Elaine's Portuguese rice dish, Jennifer's Cuban rice dish and Hector's Puerto Rican rice dish shared ingredients and also connected cultures. An illustration in Donald Crews' *Bigmamama's* touched off a cross cultural discussion about food. The picture showed a pile of cane pulp and the vat for making syrup from sugar cane juice. Cesar and Gisela were familiar with sugar cane juice from the Dominican Republic; Eve knew about it from Puerto Rico, and Wilfredo had encountered it in Honduras. I mentioned that we have a kind of counterpart here in New England with maple sugar sap; European American Peter knowledgeably described the process of boiling it down to get syrup.

We Identify U.S. Cultural Phenomena That Are Like and Unlike Those of Other Countries

There were no books about Dominicans or the Dominican Republic. This bothered me since eight of my students had been born there. I used *Josephine's 'Magination,* which takes place in Haiti, and directed students' attention to geographical descriptions similar to those of the Dominican Republic: the weather, plant and animal life, and effects of proximity to the ocean. The Dominican students recognized the similarities. Part of the story takes place in an outdoor market. Most of the Dominican students had visited a market like that described in the book, as had I. I was trying to convey some idea of what it was like to students born in the United States when Elaine began to describe the sights and smells of a tropical foods market in her neighborhood. Julia, of Costa Rican descent but born in Boston, asked about Haymarket, an outdoor market in downtown Boston, which I had forgotten. "That's the closest thing we have," I agreed. "What about flea markets?" someone asked. I was amazed. In less than a minute they had made three connections which, when pooled, gave everyone in the room a pretty good idea of what a Third World market was like!

But we also discovered some cultural phenomena that were uniquely North American. As Thanksgiving drew near, we learned that not everyone in the class was planning to celebrate the holiday, notably those who were most recently arrived. "Just like in *Molly's Pilgrim*," Jennifer said. "She didn't know about Thanksgiving either." I reminded them that it was a U.S. holiday, not celebrated in some other countries.

We Examine Values and Traditions

In December we read *The Christmas Secret*, a book I thought authentically reflected Latino values. It is the story of Jose and his younger brother, Latino boys who secretly sell Christmas trees to be able to buy a Christmas present for their mother. I asked the class what the story revealed about this family and was fascinated by the spirited exchange that took place between Latino and non-Latino students. Cesar noted that the boys helped their mother by doing the dishes and other chores. European American Katie interpreted the mother's comment that the boys help her "too much" as a complaint. Dominican Gisela vigorously objected. The boys' mother was proud, she said, that her boys could do so much. She went on to say that *her* mother felt it was important that she learn to do things because she would need to do things for herself someday. It was clear to me as I listened to them debate that Gisesla identified with that family and understood perfectly the underlying values. When the class began to discuss why Jose didn't charge a neighbor for carrying home her tree, one of the non-Latino students suggested that perhaps Jose was trying to bribe her into not revealing his secret job. Several Latino students disagreed, saying that the reason he didn't charge her was that she was a friend of the family and "you couldn't charge a friend of the family."

Flossie and the Fox, set in the rural South, illustrated other values and traditions. It is a "Little Red Riding Hood" story in which African American Flossie outwits Fox who tries to steal the basket of eggs she is talking to Miz Viola's. We noted her curtsies and politeness to her elders, including Fox. Flossie called her grandmother Big Mama. I asked the children how they addressed their grandmothers and made a list of the fifteen or so Spanish and English names they offered. I asked if, like Flossie's grandmother, any of their mothers covered their heads while they worked. African American Kamal said his mother did; I said I thought it was an African tradition. Elaine said her grandmother did, and Wilfredo, a dark-skinned Honduran, said his grandmother did, too. I sensed a desire on the part of the students to claim this African connection. Teresa, a dark-skinned girl from the Dominican Republic, said that many women in her country covered their heads. I reminded the class that many Dominicans are of African descent.

Family Stories Help Students Connect

Judy and I were ever alert for new books to support our "family stories" project. "Family stories" are stories about family members or family experiences which are told on occasions when the family gets together. They are told over and over, but no one ever gets tired of hearing them; it is as though the bonds of family members are strengthened and celebrated in the retelling. I created an illustrated, bilingual book of a funny story from my childhood which is often retold when my family gets together, and I sent home photocopies with a request that parents rehearse a story with their child which could then be written and illustrated in school.

This was only one of several projects which required the help of parents. We knew that implementing a curriculum that has as its starting point the cultural, racial and linguistic identities of students was going to require the ongoing assistance and involvement of families. Soon after school began we held an Open House to explain our program, answer questions and solicit help for our upcoming camping trip. It was my experience that parents enjoyed being called on to supply a link to the cultural heritage of their children. After interviewing her father about his childhood in rural Puerto Rico, for example, Marta reported that he had said he was "really glad they make kids do projects like these."

While children collected their family stories, I read aloud books like *Uncle's New Suit, Mack & Marie & the Train Toss Surprise, Mean Old Uncle Jack* and *Shortcut* so that they could see what other authors had done with their family stories. From the students we got some wonderful stories. Eva wrote about the day her little brother got lost at the mall. Peter recounted a fast-paced automobile trip across an Arizona desert with a broken rearview mirror and a family member who identified the police cruiser following them only as a "black and white car." Jennifer wrote about the dog who "ate our Christmas tree."

We Confront Issues of Race and Prejudice

One family story which took us to a discussion of ideas beyond family was the previously mentioned *Bigmama's* by African American author Donald Crews. It is the story of the author's trip by train to Florida during summer vacations to visit his grandparents.

I introduced the book by asking students if any of them had traveled to visit relatives. Nearly everyone had, and they told of local trips as well as trips to Florida, Puerto Rico and the Dominican Republic. But students noticed that Crews made his trip in an earlier time. Elaine's sharp eye noted the "colored" sign posted in the railroad car occupied by Donald Crews' family. We examined the date on the license plate of the car that met them at the station and noted that those trips took place long before Rosa Parks and Martin Luther King succeeded in making such discrimination illegal. Students were prompted to discuss their own experiences with discrimination. Elaine recounted being discriminated against by a cashier who took everyone else's money first. She was pretty sure it happened because she was black and the cashier was white. We discussed the possibility of age discrimination as well, since the cashier was "old." "People only like people who are like themselves," mused Julia. She had verbalized the attitude we were trying so hard to overcome. Elaine wasn't the only student who had experienced discrimination. Many of the Latino students had, too. They were mesmerized by *Felita*, the story of a New York born Puerto Rican girl. The book's theme is prejudice, directed this time against Latinos. We began to list the roots of prejudice, and I noticed that the students' suggestions corresponded closely to the list I had drawn up myself the previous year in an attempt to get a handle on the problem of racism. *Felita* was one of the most popular books we read. I saw that Cesar was rereading it at every spare moment during the day, oblivious to the activity around him. One day I asked him, "Cesar, you like that book, huh?" "Yes," he replied solemnly. "This is the first chapter book I've ever liked."

Though we talked in a matter-of-fact way about the greed, ignorance, poor self-esteem and "just plain meanness" which led to racial prejudice and discrimination, I was troubled by the enormity, the pervasiveness and the devastating effect of the problem.

My observation of Irene, one of my four African American students, fueled my concern and my motivation that we need to exercise a great deal of care when we construct a curriculum which deals with race. Irene was short and chubby, strong-willed and temperamental. Her personality was endearingly transparent. Everything she felt was immediately reflected in her facial expressions and body language and, depending on the circumstances, in irrepressible giggles or angry outbursts. Irene was smart and very ambitious. She liked being first; she liked being right; she liked being the best. If she wasn't first, right or the best, there was trouble. She once sobbed, sulked and stomped out of the room upon receiving 98% on a math test, while her peers tried in vain to convince her it was an "A."

Irene made it obvious that she did not like to dwell on slavery or on the discrimination African Americans face today. After reading *Dancing with the Indians,* I taped a discussion in which students compared the experience of Native Americans to that of African Americans. At the end Elaine speaks passionately about "where we live you see Black people not getting jobs and you see companies run by White people having better things ... you don't see Black people in cartoons..." As she speaks and after she finishes, Irene's voice is heard: "All right, Elaine. All right, Elaine. All right, Elaine, Gosh!"

When I showed a movie about Harriet Tubman with scenes of frightened slaves arguing about whether to go forward or return to the plantation, Irene lay with her legs on the chair and her head on the rug as though she didn't really want to watch. When Jefferson Davis appeared, though, and began to cooly enumerate the reasons why slavery should be retained, I heard her say quietly but intensely, "I hate him."

Irene's reactions, especially to the film, reinforced my own doubts about the appropriateness for young children of a curriculum which focuses on slavery. Who, after all, enjoys seeing one's people powerless, dependent and terror-stricken, or would like to be reminded that, while slavery is gone, de facto second-class citizenship is still a reality for most dark-skinned people? Who, especially if you are a feisty, ambitious third grader with the highest expectations for yourself? The issue was one Judy and I had to deal with because a number of our books about African Americans were set in slave times. To balance these books, we sought out others like *Mufaro's Beautiful Daughters, Masai and I* or *The Orphan Boy,* with images of Africa unrelated to slavery or stories about contemporary African American families like *The Patchwork Quilt, Three Wishes, Back Home,* or *Joshua's Masai Mask.* Whenever we dealt with slavery, we tried to stress the positive: The Africans who were enslaved possessed languages and cultures of their own; they, and their descendants, never gave up trying to regain their freedom. Irene's favorite book was *Honey I Love* by Eloise Greenfield. Her favorite poem in the collection was "Harriet Tubman" which begins "Harriet Tubman didn't take no stuff/ Wasn't scared of nothing neither. …"

The Seeds of Change Exhibit Promotes Multicultural Understanding

One way to nudge students to new perspectives is to examine how people in different situations are affected by the same events. Much of our curriculum was inspired by the "Seeds of Change" exhibit developed by the Smithsonian to coincide with the 500th anniversary of Columbus's voyages to the New World. Instead of presenting Columbus's voyages and their effects from the traditional, purely European point of view, the exhibit highlighted what was in reality a process of cultural exchange between two worlds with profound repercussions for both.

I read aloud a number of books about Columbus, including *Encounter,* a powerful and chilling account of Columbus's arrival from the point of view of a Taino Indian. I asked students to consider whether each book reflected the traditional white European point of view, the point of view of the Native Americans, or both. They did this easily, giving evidence for their opinions. After responding in this way to several books, Elaine reacted indignantly to one traditional version: "Columbus showed them what *he* had, but he didn't even notice what they had."

In November I read *How Many Days to America?* about a boatload of Caribbean refugees who, after being turned away at various ports, arrive in America on Thanksgiving Day and are warmly received. Peter told of his grandfather who had to leave Germany because of a war, and Jennifer said that was why her mother had to leave Cuba. I reluctantly informed them (noting with irony how I cling to myths) that the United States doesn't accept all the people who want to come here, that sometimes people are turned away, that some Americans think we don't have enough jobs for our own people. To my surprise (I was once more assuming that everyone thought the way I did!) that was an idea with which many of them, whose parents were struggling to earn a living, seemed to identify. Joe, of Irish descent, commented: "We were lucky to get in when we did."

We returned often to the idea that one's circumstances affect one's point of view. It was Elaine, moody and talkative but extremely insightful, who was especially adept at seeing reality from more than one perspective. Once I was reading aloud *The Picture Book of Harriet Tubman.* In this book the author makes the point that thirteen southern states were so upset by Abraham

Lincoln's election that they decided to secede from the Union. I decided an explanation was in order. "The people in those states were so opposed to Lincoln's views on slavery that they didn't want to be part of the United States anymore," I said. "The *white* people, Mrs. Miller, the *white* people in those states didn't like Lincoln's views on slavery," Elaine amended.

We Come to Respect Each Other's Language

Multicultural literature brought a variety of languages into the classroom, including that of Flossie and Big Mama in Patricia McKissack's *Flossie and the Fox*:

> *"Why come Mr. J. W. can't catch the fox with his dogs?"*
> *Flossie asked, putting a peach in her apron pocket to*
> *eat later.*
>
> *"Ever-time they corner that ol' slickster, he gets away. I tell*
> *you, that fox is one sly critter."*
>
> *"How do a fox look?" Flossie asked. "I disremember ever*
> *seeing one."*
>
> *Big Mama had to think a bit. "Chile, a fox be just a fox.*
> *But one thing for sure, that rascal loves eggs. He'll do*
> *most anything to get at some eggs."*

Irene loved the language of *Flossie and the Fox*. She sat at the front of the room and I could hear her chuckling as I read it. Once when I slipped and read "Miss Viola," she corrected me. "No, it's *Miz* Viola," she said. I was ready this year to talk about Flossie's dialect, but only after asking myself some hard questions and realizing, with shame, that way down deep I'd had doubts about the answers. I asked myself: Is Flossie's dialect inferior? Is it not as good as "standard" English? Would it be embarrassing to African American students to label it African American?

I needn't have been concerned for my students. Everyone liked the way Flossie talked. Elaine quickly informed us that Flossie's was a Southern dialect. Kamal said that his grandmother in North Carolina spoke with a Southern accent. I told them that the African slaves had come speaking the languages of West Africa, like Ibo, and that they learned English by hearing it spoken.

European American Peter said that he talked like Fox. At first I thought he was rejecting Flossie's speech, but then I realized that he really did have an affected "cultured" way of talking. Irene said that her mother talked like Fox, too, when she was on the telephone. I told them that we had Boston accents and sounded strange to people in other parts of the country. I could see that was a new thought. They considered it for several moments in silence.

The school year sped along, filled with books and activities which encouraged students to take pride in their own cultures and use them as stepping stones to academic achievement, while learning to understand and appreciate the cultures of their classmates. On the last day of the school year, I invited the parents to a final celebration, reminding them in the invitation of the important role they had played in their children's educational experience during the year. Though only ten families were able to make it, each of those arrived with, it seemed, no less than three family members. The classroom was packed; the *flan* and *arroz con leche* were flowing. About half the class volunteered to read aloud one of the stories in the books they had made. Many chose to read a story about the childhood of a parent who was present. We listened to accounts of growing up in Cuba; in Roxbury and Everett, Massachusetts; in Puerto Rico and the Dominican Republic. Some of the children read about funny events in their families' lives. Then I presented an award to each child for something at which he or she had excelled during the year. The audience applauded enthusiastically for every one of them, and I heard frequent exclamations of "I knew it!" as Joaquin was named "Class Artist" and Jennifer was named "Best Writer," etc. Finally, it was time to dance. The merengue tape was produced and Alejandro, who had been known to "dance" a merengue while seated, got his chance to perform. And then there were hugs, kisses, a few tears, and it was over.

Did I achieve my goals? Did the children learn more as a result of pursuing a curriculum which met them where they were racially, culturally and linguistically? Had they glimpsed that there were other, equally valid points of view out there? Certainly there had been achievement, and enthusiasm, and evidence that they had expanded their horizons.

I thought of Gisela and Jennifer, who had taught themselves to read in Spanish, and of Irene's progress in speaking Spanish, a quest she abandoned only when steeping herself joyfully in the poetry of Langston Hughes and Eloise Greenfield.

I thought of Rosa, completing her first school year in the United States, flushed and smiling as she accepted a special award commemorating her passion for learning.

Language had been no barrier to friendship for Teresa, who had been one of Irene's most patient Spanish teachers and had learned a lot of English in the process. Puerto Rican Eva told me that she had enjoyed learning African American history and tiny Noemi, who decided on her own to repeat third grade, confided that she liked teaching Spanish to her classmates. Fernando, who had begun the year insisting that he could not understand a word of English, ended it indignant that he had not received English reading instruction in second grade.

I knew, however, that I had been about the business of planting seeds, and I would never know with certainty the extent to which I had met my goals. Of Judy's growth and my own growth I could be more certain. Judy came away with new strategies for teaching limited-English-proficient students in the regular education classroom. Books in her students' first languages would always be part of her classroom library; children would be encouraged to speak and to write in their first languages as well as in English. It wasn't necessary, she realized, that she understand every story shared by student authors; there would always be students willing and able to translate when it was important to do so.

For myself, the wrenching lessons of the previous year had served me well, though I had by no means "arrived," as some of the incidents I have recounted demonstrate. I had a better grasp of the power and pervasiveness of culture and knew that, like it or not, I would always be to some extent a prisoner of my own culture. Would that there were a student like Elaine in every future class to remind me of that fact. I knew that I would continue to address issues of race and culture ever more directly and confidently, even if I went back, as I did, to teaching exclusively Latino bilingual classes. In the course of the year I had come to realize that my newly-arrived Latino students had some very special needs which, given the lack of support services, could probably best be met in the traditional, substantially separate bilingual class. Though I knew that I would always seek opportunities to bring my students into contact with children of other linguistic and cultural traditions, I came to realize that they, who shared the Boston neighborhoods of Jamaica Plain and Roxbury with children of other languages and cultures, were far less isolated than I. Never again would I assume that I could supply everything my students needed. In the fall, I would enlist the help of the Dominican paraprofessional to provide a much needed Dominican perspective for our curriculum. I would reach out to African American teachers in my new school for help in celebrating Kwanzaa. After all, we had African roots to celebrate, too. Two years earlier, I hadn't listened when an African American colleague warned me that my curriculum was "too white." Now I was listening.

References

Anancy and Mr. Dry Bone. Fiona French. Little, Brown & Co. Boston, 1991.

Anansi the Spider. Gerald McDermott. Henry Holt and Company. New York, 1972. (paperback)

Back Home. Gloria Jean Pinkney. Dial Books for Young Readers. New York, 1992.

Bigmama's. Donald Crews. Greenwillow Books. New York, 1991.

The Christmas Secret, Joan Lexau. Scholastic, Inc. (paperback originally published by Dial Books for Young Readers. New York, 1963.)

Cornrows. Camille Yarbrough. Coward-McCann, Inc. New York, 1979.

Dancing with the Indians. Angela Medearis. Holiday. New York, 1991.

Dragonfly's Tale. Kristina Rodanas. Clarion Books. New York, 1991.

Encounter. Jane Yolen. Harcourt Brace Jovanovich. New York, 1992.

Felita. Nicholasa Mohr. A Bantam Skylark Book. New York, 1979. (paperback)

Flossie & the Fox. Patricia G. McKissack. Dial Books for Young Readers. New York, 1986.

Honey I Love: and Other Love Poems. Eloise Greenfield. Crowell Junior Books. New York, 1978.

How Many Days to America? A Thanksgiving Story. Eve Bunting. Clarion Books. New York, 1988.

Josephine's 'magination. Arnold Dobrin. Scholastic, Inc. New York, 1973. (paperback)

Joshua's Masai Mask. Dakari Hru. Lee & Low Books. New York, 1993.

Mac & Marie & the Train Toss Surprise. Elizabeth Fitzgerald Howard. Four Winds Press. New York, 1993.

Masai and I. Virginia Kroll. Four Winds Press. New York, 1992.

Mean Old Uncle Jack. Anna Grossnickle Hines. Clarion Books. New York, 1990.

Molly's Pilgrim. Barbara Cohen. Lothrop, Lee & Shepard Books. New York, 1983.

Mufaro's Beautiful Daughters: An African Tale. John Steptoe. Lothrop, Lee & Shepard Books. New York, 1987.

Night on Neighborhood Street. Eloise Greenfield. Dial Books for Young Readers. New York, 1991.

Rainbow Crow. Nancy Van Laan. Alfred A. Knopf. New York, 1989.

Shortcut. Donald Crews. Greenwillow Books. New York, 1992.

Song of the Chirimia. Jane Anne Volkmer. Carolrhoda Books. Minneapolis, 1990.

The Orphan Boy. Tololwa M. Mollel. Clarion Books. New York, 1990.

The Patchwork Quilt. Valerie Flournoy. Dial Books for Young Readers. New York, 1985.

The Picture Book of Harriet Tubman. David A. Adler. Holiday. New York, 1992.

Three Wishes. Lucille Clifton. A Doubleday Book for Young Readers. New York, 1992.

Uncle's New Suit. Lisa Passen. Henry Holt and Company. New York, 1992.

Yagua Days. Cruz Martel. Dial Books for Young Readers. New York, 1976.

Poems and Legends
"Buenos Vecinos." In *Dias y Dias de Poesia.* Alma Flor Ada. Hampton-Brown Books. Carmel, California, 1991.

"Why Corn Has Silky White Hair." In *Hidden Stories in Plants.* Anne Pellowski. Macmillan Publishing Company. New York, 1990.

Dialogue Journals:

Passing Notes the Academic Way

by

CHRISTINE CZIKO

My name is Carlos. I'm in Ms. Cziko's first period. I am fifteen and a-half years old and I hate school. I liked the first chapter to this book and I'll think that I will enjoy the rest of the book. And I also hate school. I hate it so much that I had to mention it twice. But then who doesn't?

 HEN students are lined up, searched, and ordered into classrooms each day, the message is pretty clear. They are unwelcome at best and assumed to be criminal at worst. Control becomes the most compelling lesson of the school day. Even within classrooms a "pedagogy of control" — worksheets, copying from the board, multiple-choice tests, assigned compositions — seems to many teachers the most appropriate way to teach in this setting. To some it is nothing less than a survival strategy.

For the last 12 years of my 20-year career teaching English in New York City junior and senior high schools, I have been struggling to find ways to actively engage my students in reading and writing. I have turned away from "objective" questions and answers about literature to reader response logs. I have stopped using grammar texts in favor of a process approach to writing. I don't assign research papers but instead try to engage kids in critical inquiry leading to "I-Search" papers. I've replaced tests with portfolios. In short, I've tried to put the student at the center of his or her own learning. It has been an uphill journey. When teachers invite students to be active learners in a school like mine, it's no surprise that the invitation is looked upon with distrust.

Yo, my name is Awilda and I don't like this book. It a wasts of my damn time. I'm in Ms. C. class 6 period. If I read this book it because they force me.

I teach in an inner city, comprehensive high school of over 4,000 students, 99% of whom are African American, Caribbean or Hispanic. The school is dirty, overcrowded and sometimes dangerous. There are 17 full-time security guards who use metal detectors to search students and scan their bookbags for weapons as they enter the building each day. There are 10 deans who use bull horns in the hallways to order kids to class or race to the scene of fights called in regularly on their walkie-talkies. The attendance is low, the dropout rate is high and the morale is near zero for both students and staff.

In a dehumanizing environment like this one, many students become either passive or actively hostile. Hostile students spend much of their time in the dean's office, on suspension, roaming the hallways or simply cutting school. The majority of students try to find ways to get through the day, get through the term, get through school and get out.

For a number of years I had been asking students to write "literature logs" — personal responses to books we were reading in class. The results were mixed. Students who already liked to read seemed to enjoy writing in their logs and often wrote many pages of personal reactions to the books. In these cases, the problem became my inability to respond to their writing. With five classes of over 30 students per class, if only half of my students wrote in their logs, I had 80 students to write back to. As a result, a real "conversation" about the book wasn't possible, and some students complained that they were just writing to themselves.

The more serious problem was those students who just didn't read. Many of my students find reading a task with few rewards. Some have never read a complete book and lacked both the confidence and motivation to try. They were also put off by the solitary nature of reading. Clearly students couldn't create meanings or become engaged in texts that they didn't read. These students' literature logs remained blank.

> *What's up. I'm Eddie. What's up Felix and Carlos. I hope yarl follow my footsteps. Anyway, the story wasn't so bad in the beginning but I don't like it. I don't like to read period besides the fact that its boring or not boring. I hate to read. I will read but reading and I don't get along.*

> *My name is Curtis. I'm in Ms. Cziko's eight period class. ... Between you and me, Jackie, I never read a whole book before.*

What I needed was a way to get kids reading, and then engage them in ongoing and authentic conversations about their response to what they read. I knew that social concerns were high on my students list of priorities. It was in social settings that they came to life — you could feel the energy and excitement in the halls, the cafeteria, the schoolyard — while the classrooms were dead. School itself was seen by most of my students as a primarily social institution.

> *Anyone going to the Evander dance tonight? Well I am. You might see me. Today I have on an orange ACA Joe sweatshirt, purple Guess jeans and brown, orange and purple Nike A.C.G.'s. I might have on my glasses and my ponytail is to the side. I'm kind of tan and you can't miss me, so if anyone sees me ya'll could say hi!*
> *Rhonda AKA Ron-du*

I had to find a way to build on kids' social interests — to connect what I wanted kids to do with what they wanted to do. I had to figure out how to engage students in ways that met both their academic and social needs.

At a workshop sponsored by the NYC Writing Project, I heard Dixie Goswami describe a journal writing activity that one of the Breadloaf teachers, Dale Lumley, was using in his classes. He called it peer dialogue journals. Students from one class were paired with students in another class who were reading the same books. The students carried on a written dialogue in a shared journal about what they were reading.

The idea seemed to be just what I was looking for, though I realized from the start that I would have to adapt the activity to make it work in my urban school. First, I would have to get the materials — the school wouldn't provide the journals, and it was unlikely that students who often came to class without notebooks or paper would buy their own logs. Since we did have loose leaf paper and I owned a stapler, I enlisted a few volunteers to staple together 30 sets of 12-page "logs." These logs were also easily transportable — a necessity when you must move from classroom to classroom to meet your students each day.

Second, I realized that I couldn't simply partner students in my ninth grade classes. With an average daily absentee rate of over 30%, many kids would end up with their partners absent on any given day.

> *I don't know what's going on in the book because I've been absent. I haven't really read but I'll catch up.*
> *Thomas*

> *Nobody hasn't written so far. I guess everyone is absent today. I hate writing to myself or answering myself. Well, at least I know I'm passing.... Melissa*

So I decided to group four students in each log — one from each of my ninth grade English classes.

Finally, I had to get a book that I thought students would find interesting to read. I chose *The Pigman* by Paul Zindel. Though its main characters are white, suburban and middle class, I hoped that the humor in the book — as well as the universal concern of teenagers with issues of identity, conflicts with parents and relationships with the opposite sex — would engage my students even though they were black and Hispanic, urban and working class or poor. Besides, it was the only ninth grade novel available to me in sufficient numbers for four classes to read at the same time.

> *My name is Tyrone. This story is dumb. It is confusing the way they talk about things. The curse words he should had left in the story to make it more exciting. Peace with chicken grease!*

> *Hello, my name is Khalilah. I thought the story was OK. I like the way John describes his feelings. From what I have read it seems like it may be an interesting story. ...*

> *Peace. I read chapter 1, 2 and 3 and I still think its a*
> *boring book because its not real. I only like gangster stories*
> *so this book isn't for me. Peace.*
>   *Andrew*

During the three weeks that it took us to read *The Pigman*, students wrote willingly in their journals and eagerly read the writing of their partners. I did not "teach" the book with questions and answers or class discussions centered on what I thought was important. I did create a list of writing activities, separate from the dialogue journals, that invited students to write about events in their own lives that paralleled events in the book (the death of a friend, a first kiss, a party that got out of control). Other than that, what I provided was a timetable — which chapters to read by when — and a structure for class time.

Each day students could spend time reading their journals and answering their partners, working on their writing activities or reading the novel itself. An occasional "reading check" (credit or no credit for keeping up) gave the more reluctant readers an extra push. Discussion of the book took place among students solely within the pages of their journals. I served as advisor, mentor and cheerleader.

I gave my students few guidelines for their journal entries, except that they had to write something about the book each time they wrote. At times, conversations in the journals became so social that the book was almost forgotten. Once, after about a week of writing, I asked students to either ask their partners a question or answer a question their partners had about the book.

> *Hi, its me again, Joel. … I have a few questions. Why did*
> *the Pigman let John and Lorraine in his house at the be-*
> *ginning of the book, and why did he work himself out and*

nearly have a heart attack? And why did he let John and Lorraine use his house? Why does the Pigman trust John and Lorraine so much?

Joel, he probably trust them so much because he is lonely. And he would probably trust anybody right now. ...
    Felicia

Hello, its Danny. I agree with Felicia, Joel. He trust them so much because he is lonely. And they did make good friends. Sometimes when people get old they have to have an anchor to help them keep in touch with reality. They were his anchor and his second trip to youth.

As I had hoped, real conversations about ideas, inspired by reading, were happening in the logs. They weren't happening for everyone or all the time — but when they did happen, there was an authenticity that had been missing in most of the "class discussions" I had tried to initiate in other classes at other times. Students were admitting confusions...

Hi everybody! I have completed the reading of chapters 14 and 15 but I really did not understand the ending of chapter 15. Why? I don't know, but it seemed a little too confusing for me. Could one of you girls explain it for me? Thanks! Bye People!!!
    Roy

I also thought the ending of chapter 15 was confusing. This is to Roy — I thought that at the end of chapter 15 John was thinking and talking about how peoples' lives are like cages. We only have so much space and we must make the best out of it for everyone. ...
    Latasha

they were defending opinions…

> *Hi, its me Joel. … I agree that John and Lorraine did take advantage of the Pigman. But, I feel that it's not Lorraine and John's fault for the Pigman's death. The Pigman should have known that he is an old man, maybe he feels or thinks he's young, but he can't do things that young people can do. … In other words, make believe John and Lorraine represent a gun salesman. Now the gun salesman sells a gun to the Pigman. Let's say the gun represents fun. Now if the Pigman uses the gun (fun) but kills himself with it, who's fault is it? The gun salesman (John and Lorraine) or the one who used the gun?*

and they were exploring their feelings as they read together…

> *I finished reading the book and I thought it was good. John and I relatively feel the same way about death, sometimes I really do feel the same way he does, I feel like if death is going to take me, take me now, don't wait so long.*
> *Joanne*

But more happened in these logs than I had anticipated. As a teacher I had my own intentions for the writing — academic intentions. I wanted students to explore theme, analyze character, make predictions — all the stuff that would make me feel like I was being a "real English teacher." Yes, these kinds of discussions were happening, but my students also had other ideas, their own intentions. They were building social communities within the pages of these logs, communities in which they argued, encouraged, flirted, apologized, advised, and confided. They were using writing as a tool for knowing and connecting to each other in a school environment where most felt anonymous and alone.

Awilda, I am sorry if I kinda dissed you about youre hand-writing. I hope you accept my forgiveness. James, you so right about what you said about I shouldn't have tell Awilda about her handwriting. Vito, I don't hear too much from you but you still my friend.
Trina

If you look good, Khalilah, why don't you write your phone number so my man can call you.
Omar

Charlene, I know your vex with me. I like the Bulls that my choose. You like the Knicks and that your choose.
Tameca

Tameca, I'm sorry about what happened. I like the Bulls and the Knicks but it just annoys me that everytime I try to talk to you, you have an attitude....
Charlene

What'sup, it Eileen. ...By the way Tameca and Charlene, both of you have attitudes, so stop it.

Within their dialogue journals, my students interacted socially in writing. The immediate feedback they received from each other encouraged them to keep writing and to keep reading. Reading, in fact, became a required activity in order to participate fully in this new and interesting social setting.

I enjoyed writing in the log. That's actually the only reason why I read the story. It wasn't a lot of effort put into this log but at least we did communicate. Bye.
Tawana

The logs provided students with a place where it was "cool" for them to talk to each other about literature — conversations which often can't be initiated by kids among their peers without risking adolescent scorn.

> *I really didn't write much about the story. But I read all of the entries you guys had written and they were very funny. You all sound like cool people. And I should had made more responses to all of you.*
> *Peace out Jason*

> *I enjoy having like a writing pen pal. The book was interesting and so were the comments in this log. … I ready to read another short book. As long as its short,*
> *Sincerely, Eddie*

At the end of three weeks we had finished reading the book, and I decided to ask students to write a final entry in their logs. It was the end of May, the term would be over soon, and though I felt that something exciting had been happening during these last few weeks, I was eager to actually read the logs to find out what it was.

> *Well I've just finished reading The Pigman. I have enjoyed it. … Oh! last but not least, it was really fun writing to you all, and even though we're finished reading the book it would be nice if we can still write to each other, saying what we are doing in Ms. Cziko's class. Goodbye! Everyone!!*
> *Felicia*

> *Hi everyone. Here are just a few lines to let you know I enjoyed having the opportunity to write my comments and opinions in this log with you. I hope you all enjoyed the book like I did. I think more teachers should do things like*

*this more often. ... Well now is the time to say goodbye to
all of you. Goodbye and keep up the good work in Ms.
Cziko's class.*
  Latasha

*Well, hi again girls. This is our final writing and I think
I'm going to miss you guys writing to me. But I'll see you
around. I am going to miss Eileen with her words, the way
she said them. And Charlene, miss you because the Bulls
win and we can't argue over nothing. I don't know nothing
about Diana. But it was nice having you guys as a friend.
Bye Eileen, Charlene and Diana.*
  Tameca

*Dear Jaclyn,
I'm afraid this has to be the last entry in the log. I've had fun
writing to you and I hope you enjoyed writing to me. Although
we never saw each other I feel we have known each other all
our lives. It is not easy to tell someone who you never met
anything about yourself, but, somehow, I found it easy to do. I
really admire you and respect you, Jaclyn. Who knows, maybe
someday I'll stop by your gym class.*
  Your friend, Curtis

My mind is filled with ideas — and with questions. I've already
begun dialogue journals with my new group of ninth grade students, but I don't want to simply repeat what I did before. I
want to find ways to help students build on the private conversations that occurred between them in their logs so that they
can enter into more public discussions — public writing —
through which they will learn to present their ideas to a broader
audience. I want to help my students "go public" with what
they think, both in form and content, without losing their authentic voices.

I know that I helped create an environment in my ninth grade classes in which the necessary first step of engagement could take place — necessary but not sufficient. This term I plan to take a more active role in the dialogue journals. I'm reluctant to enter directly into journal conversations. I don't want to upset these tentative learning communities with my loud "teacher voice." But I will, with students' permission, bring to whole classes the issues and debates that emerge in the journals. I hope to help students begin to find more public forums for the ideas that spring from social conversations and private concerns.

In an odd way I've circled back to where I began. How do I continue to find ways to connect my academic intentions for students with the private and social intentions they hold for themselves? Dialogue journals seem to me to be one bridge across this chasm. I continue to look for others.

One thing, though, is clear to me. Finding ways to connect students' social interests to academic intentions can result in powerful learning — learning that engages both the mind and the heart.

Looking at Community

Looking at Community

Schools thrive when they build bridges to the families and communities they serve. When teachers and parents communicate, they take a giant step toward improving the learning opportunities for children. However, in modern urban settings where parents often work long hours and late shifts, traditional methods of school-family communication — the PTA meeting, the parent teacher conference, for instance — become hard to pull off. The teachers writing in this section — Marci Resnick, Deborah Jumpp and Carole Chin — refuse to be deterred by these handicaps. They have worked out creative and effective ways of establishing bonds with the people and communities that matter in the lives of their students.

Making Connections Between Families and School

by

<small>Marci Resnick</small>

**F**OR most of the 18 years I have taught at my Philadelphia elementary school, the same sign has been fastened to an easel just inside the school's entrance: PARENTS — REPORT TO THE OFFICE FIRST — IT'S THE LAW. Each morning I have walked heedlessly by this sign. But on one particular morning the sign spoke to me in a new way. On that morning the sign was to become a symbol of the mixed messages schools send to parents about their roles in their children's education. I started to think about how that sign, present in most schools throughout the city, represented all the work that was needed in order to improve the relationship between families and schools.

I do not believe I would have come to see the sign in this way if I had not become involved with the Urban Sites Network of the National Writing Project. As a participant in the Network, I began to look for ways to build connections between my classroom, my students and their families. In the process, I paid attention to what I was doing: I kept a journal, collected student work, logged conversations with parents, and conducted end-of-the-year surveys of students and their families.

Also during this time, the third grade team of teachers at my school began implementing a literature-based language arts program. This study details how my thinking about connections with families and with literature became integrated as I pursued my teacher inquiry project on relationships between families and schools.

I began my inquiry project in a school with a population of one thousand kindergarten to fourth grade students. The student population was 98 percent African American; the teaching staff was 60 percent African American and 40 percent European American. Mostly working families lived in the neighborhood surrounding the school, many of whom had been hit hard by the loss of industrial jobs in Philadelphia. The school building was 75 years old and, as is the case with such aging buildings, we sometimes taught while asbestos was being removed and contained, when we were without heat or had too much heat, and when there were no working water fountains.

Conversations with Parents:
Talking Together about Learning

During the school day there is little time for teachers to connect with the families of their students, unless an emergency occurs. Early on in my teaching career, I began calling parents on a monthly basis at home in the evenings because I was having a hard time bringing out the best in the children in my classroom. I thought that the very act of calling homes would motivate students to do better. In fact, it did have a very positive effect in the classroom. So I continued making these supportive though minimal contacts with families during all of my years of teaching.

When I participated in the Philadelphia Writing Project's Summer Institute several years ago, I had time to reflect on my work and think about the importance of building connections to families. I once again considered the phone calls I had been making to parents. I began seeing them not only as a way to give information to parents, but also as a way to receive a more complete picture of each child. The conversations became a way to forge a relationship with the parents of my students as I shared stories about my own family and children, and they shared stories and information about theirs.

Most of these shared telephone stories had to do with everyday issues we'd faced as parents and workers. Some of them revealed a similar way of looking at things. For example, Barry's mother and I spent much time talking about how to set limits for our children and how hard that can be. Other conversations reminded me of the possibility of making different meaning out of the same situation. One example I documented involved a phone conversation I had with Andrew's mother in October 1991. I worried about Andrew's seriousness which I just assumed was based on something going on at home, school or both. He never smiled or seemed to be enjoying himself. I was concerned that he didn't seem to appreciate the class. A phone conversation with his mother reminded me of the dangers of making such assumptions. She related to me that she tells Andrew every day to take school seriously. She wants no playing around. She values his education and wants him to value it as well. I learned something about Andrew's family and their values and priorities. I saw Andrew's seriousness in a new way.

I noted the content of these phone calls in my journal which I kept throughout the two years of my inquiry project. At the beginning of my journal are references to a series of phone calls I shared with Donald's aunt, Mrs. Johnson. Donald was still a beginning reader in the third grade, and our calls in October were about his reading. Mrs. Johnson planned to go to the library and take out books we had read in class like *Abiyoyo* and *Bringing the Rain to Kapiti Plain*. We talked about how Donald dictated stories to her at home and how we could then practice reading them. She told me about his strengths, particularly in math, and the need for me to foster these skills to help build his confidence and self-esteem which had been badly shaken.

Later, when the class wrote family stories, Donald's aunt helped him write a powerful story about his grandmother and grandfather:

Donald's Family Story
Once upon a time there was a large family. Their name was Richardson. The mother was called Momma Richardson and the father was called Daddy Richardson. No one could remember their first names because there were so many of them. One day they had to move out of the house where they lived because the rent was too high. So they moved to a new house on 29th Street. Next door lived a lady named Miss Janey. She was very mean. She thought there were too many children and she didn't think Momma Richardson would keep a clean house with so many children. She wouldn't speak to Momma Richardson. She wouldn't let them sit on her steps. She was just plain old mean. She told others about the family. But one day Miss Janey lost her

keys to her house and couldn't get in her front door. So guess who she had to get? One of the Richardson kids climbed in a second floor window from their roof to let her in her house. Ever since, she treated all the children nice, even Momma. She also found out Momma Richardson was a very good housekeeper. She said one day when they were all sitting outside on the steps "If there is not enough room you can sit over here on my steps." And from that day on everybody Miss Janey talked to she always said good things about Momma Richardson. She says my neighbor had fourteen children and you should see how clean and pretty her house is.

Momma Richardson and Daddy Richardson are my grandmom and grandpop and the thirteen children were my aunts and uncles. One of the children was my mom, Barbara Ann Richardson.

Written by Donald Richardson and told to him by his aunt.

She used this story to help Donald read and write and — most importantly — to feel proud of who he was. In February, Donald wrote a biography about his brother. The story tells as much about Donald's growing confidence as it does about his brother:

My brother is eleven years old. He likes to play a game called Game Boy. He likes to play football and baseball. I like to write my own story. I like to read my own story. I like to read about myself.

by Donald

Another parent and I had an extended series of conversations about reading. In the following journal entry I describe these exchanges:

After several conversations spread out over the first semester of school, I spoke with Lauren's mom, Mrs. Barnes, again. All three of us, Mrs. Barnes, Lauren and I know that she is a beginning reader. Phonetic instruction has not been helpful to her. We're all worried about her reading. Her mom says that hearing and reading the same story works best at home. She also loves to read to her younger nephew. I commented that I have been noticing that many readings of a story help Lauren.

We decided to take certain steps to help Lauren with her reading. I said I'd put stories from the classroom on tape for Lauren to use at school and home. Mrs. Barnes said she'd follow this up at home. She would also occasionally help Lauren choose books from home she's familiar with to bring to school for self-reflected reading. In class, I asked Lauren to choose a partner to echo read with her; read a line and have Lauren repeat it. Lauren seems to love to do this. I recently asked students how they think they learned to read or become better readers. Lauren said that echo reading and reading the same story have helped her most. I've noticed that in just a week's time Lauren has begun to volunteer to read aloud and complains when not given a chance to read.

Lauren began the year having difficulty reading simple books with two or three sentences on the page. By the end of the year, she could comfortably read short stories and was motivated to read longer "chapter books."

In June I asked students and parents to complete a survey on our reading program so it could be improved for the following year. In response to the questions, "What did you notice about your child's attitude and ability toward reading? Did anything change from the beginning of the year to the end of the year? If so, what?" Mrs. Barnes wrote: "Lauren started loving to read. She loves finding what is going to happen next."

Lauren wrote in a response to a similar question:

> *I did not know how to read some books that I thought were going to be hard. I learned to read more. Now sometimes I think I'll be able to read a book.*

I would like to think that the information Mrs. Barnes and I shared played a part in Lauren's new outlook towards reading and her reading development.

One thing that stood out for me about many of my phone conversations with parents was how often books and stories became the topic of our discussions. Our conversations began to have an influence on the classroom curriculum and my individual plans and goals for children.

One of the purposes for my initial school year phone call, in fact, was to find out about the interests of my students and how they could be honored in the classroom. It was these phone calls that informed me about Andrew's love of science, Jonathan's interest in computers, Lynda's use of journal writing to help control her temper, and Shonda's desire to read chapter books. While I unfortunately didn't act on all of this information, I was able, over time, to use it to enhance children's learning. Andrew became an avid observer of our monarch caterpillars, chrysalis, and finally butterflies. Shonda was encouraged at school now as well as home to read and talk about chapter books. And on numerous occasions, Lynda was encouraged to use her journal to help express angry feelings and hurtful experiences.

Parents as Resources: Bringing the Culture of the Community into the Classroom

In the Philadelphia Writing Project Summer Institute, I began reading, thinking, and having conversations about the relationship between school and culture. I started to think about how "culture" at my school seemed, for many members of the staff, to be defined as something outside of the students and their families. Culture was the study of *famous* African Americans. Students learned about their heritage through beautiful and richly informative hallway displays on Africa and historic African American figures. They learned by being encouraged to participate in writing and oratorical contests and through literature and other curriculum areas. All of these were seen as important and positive by our staff.

Yet we seemed to ignore the wealth of culture present in our own school community. We did not look to parents as a resource. There had not been an evening meeting for parents in at least twelve years. I was painfully aware that at a meeting held for parents of third grade students during the day, only two of eight staff members who were supposed to attend were actually able to do so because of difficulties presented by the school schedule. I wondered and worried about what messages these and other similar occurrences presented to parents. It occurred to me that even those of us working in schools with the best of intentions may bring with us our own assumptions about families, race, and class which may also help to create the barriers between schools and families. Particularly, as a white teacher, I wondered what I could do to include the culture of families in the classroom, as well as the culture of the world, and how to make connections between the two.

With this concern in mind, I began the school year with very definite assignments for family projects. In fact, I had a folder of these assignments ready for each child. The following is an example of an assignment from the folder:

> *Many times there are stories that have been told in families throughout the years. Maybe your great-grandmother told your grandmother a story she told your mother and your mom told it to you.*

> *See if there is a story like that in your family by asking your parents and grandparents, or another relative. Listen to the story again and write it here. Your due date is:*

At our first Urban Sites Network meeting in Philadelphia, I shared my thoughts and ideas for my teacher inquiry project. My colleagues helped me to see that this folder could not be used as I originally intended. It did not take into account who my students would be, what their interests were, and what else we would be doing in the classroom. This realization had a significant effect on my work.

Here is the revised letter which actually was sent home to parents as a result of the discussion in the Urban Sites group:

> *Dear Parents,*
> *The students from room 217 have been listening to stories from* The People Could Fly, American Black Folktales *told by Virginia Hamilton. We're talking about storytelling and how cultures tell stories. We've discussed how stories are passed from parent to child and how these are often family stories. These stories might be made-up or true accounts about the family — funny or serious.*

> *I'm hoping that you'll help your child write one of your family stories to share with the class. Like our interview*

book, I'd like to make a book of Family Stories, written and illustrated by the families of 217.

Thanks, Marci Resnick

The first letter suggests that the idea of writing family stories is an isolated one. In fact, when I wrote that letter in the summer, I wasn't thinking about the other events in the classroom that would establish the context for these stories. As the literature program in the classroom began to flourish, I immediately began to see ways to make Family Stories more than an exercise or assignment. They became a way to use home literacy to deepen and enrich our learning at school. The second letter made the connection between what we were doing at school and Family Stories, establishing a context for both. The letter also refers to the past classroom practice of publishing children's work.

So I began to see that it was the books we were reading that gave projects like writing family stories, creating family trees, and writing family recipes and family biographies their meaning.

The chart on pages 126 & 127, covering one month, illustrates how I worked on the connection between classroom reading and writing and families. The first column includes the literacy events occurring in the classroom; the next column records connections I tried to make with families. In the third column I write about the responses of families, and in last column I reflect on the process.

In selecting literature for our reading program, the third grade teachers chose children's books which represented a variety of cultures, genres, and time periods. We shared ideas for making each book a rich experience for our students. The books we read also began to help me find other ways to invite families into the classroom. For example, in the beginning of the school year we read many different fairy tales and folk tales. Parents were invited to come to school to share their favorite fairy tale with the class. Katrina's mom, Mrs. Williams, did so and continued to come to school to share books and stories with us throughout the year.

This journal entry was written after Mrs. William's second visit to the classroom in October:

> Katrina's mom, Mrs. Williams, came today with a book called Africa Adorned. It's a beautiful book. She had chosen a few pictures to show the class and began a discussion about different African tribes. It was really fascinating. The children were particularly interested at first in the lack of clothes in some of the pictures. But they got over the giggles and compared the dress to that of the Vietnamese children in the book Angel Child, Dragon Child which we recently read. Mrs. Williams promised to come back with the same book. The students will write questions they have in their response logs and will share the job finding the answers with Mrs. Williams.

> I was excited that the students compared the illustrations of clothing in Angel Child, Dragon Child with the photographs in Africa Adorned. I saw the students making connections between the classroom literature program and books shared outside of the classroom. This visit also led me to a better understanding of how my teacher inquiry project was helping to deepen my thinking about new ways for parents to be involved in the classroom.

In reflecting more about Mrs. Williams' visit in my journal, I wrote:

SEPTEMBER, 1991

Classroom Description	Connections With Family
Our focus in reading was fairy tales and folk tales. As a whole class we read: Stories From Many Lands, Abiyoyo, Lon Po Po, Mufaro's Beautiful Daughters, Ming Lo Moves Mountains. Smaller groups read Tikki Tikki Tembo, Bringing the Rain to Kapiti Plain. Individuals read many other traditional fairy tales. All students were assigned to write one fairy tale, although much of their writing in their writing folders (self-selected topics) reflected many elements of a fairy tale or a folk tale. This was seen in October newsletter, and notes on sharing time. (see attached observation for example) Students wrote at least 3 times a week for an extended period on own topics. Sharing time everyday (about 6 children). On his/her day to share, child gets a chance to share (tell about) just about anything; toys, dreams, jokes, weekend events, etc. In Science we did a butterfly project and students jotted observations daily. For Soc. St., students chose folk tale we read and found out some interesting facts about country it came from. Parents were asked to help. 13 Boys 12 Girls + 1 (new admit)	① I initiated phone calls with 15 families. The purposes were to introduce myself, open lines of communication, share information about child. I was able to reach 15 families by phone and spoke with 10 at school; (private appointments and back to school night.) (all homes were called but I was unsuccessful in reaching 10) ② We made a bulletin board for pictures of family and friends. Encouraged family connections at Sharing Time. ③ I invited parents to come to the classroom and read or tell their favorite fairy tale or folk tale. (see attached note.) ④ There was a back to school night where 8 parents came. I extended invitation to parents to read to class here, also. ⑤ I sent an introductory note home to parents. (see attached) ⑥ Began to identify children who talked about feeling upset with some aspect of what was going on at home. (See journal 9/13-91)

Two parents came to read to the class; William's and Tiana's mothers.

William appeared to be uncomfortable with his mother's visit. (see journal 9-26) This led me to have some conversations with students which I taped on how they'd like to see their parents and other family members involved in their school. (It struck me how it never occurred to me to do this earlier.)

Tiana's mom brought a book about farm animals but mostly talked with the class about growing up on a farm (see journal, 10-18) She came a few days later with a book called Africa Adorned. (see journal 10-21)

My journal entry on 10-28 talks about some reflections on these visits and how I need to think about my reactions in relationship to my own assumptions and biases.

Kashima's mom came to see me to let me know she didn't feel comfortable reading to the class but would like to volunteer 1 day a week in the classroom.

After initial phone call with Carlos' mom, she came to see me next day to talk about some anticipated family problems and their effects on Carlos

I received critical information about most students on first phone calls, ie. Direll hadn't spent full year in school yet.

What seems most important to change here, is instead of giving parents only one way in to classroom (invitation to read), I need to give many different ways for parents to become involved. Kashima's mom felt able to state her discomfort with invitation. I wonder if others felt the same way, (Ex: volunteer 1 am or pm a week, or month; Generate things adults might want to teach class; ask parents to come once a month for specific task like help in publishing)

I also need to do much better follow up with parents reading when applicable. for example, Tiana's mom began 2 excellent lessons on farms and different cultures in Africa. I lost teachable moments by not pursuing. This year I not only should pursue but let parent know how it was pursued.

These are genuine ways of looking at fact that parents want to be involved and how to build upon that involvement.

Send student invitations for Back to School Tonight saying what I'll be talking about.

Spoke to Latasha's mom and Brandon's Grandmother about home situations.

Responses	Implications / Changes

*I'm critical of myself for trying to take over Mrs. Williams'
lesson at one point. When the children started to ask her questions about the book she brought, I found myself wanting to
jump in and help answer them although Mrs. Williams didn't
need any help at all.*

This entry raised some issues for me about being a teacher. One
had to do with power and giving that up as I opened the classroom
not just to parents, but to students as well. Also, working so closely
with parents in my classroom was new for me. I was still learning
when to offer help and when to move aside. I am continuing to
think about how to help parents feel comfortable in my classroom
and how I will know when they are comfortable.

Perhaps it is the following reflection that best describes how
books provided a natural invitation for families to participate in
the classroom. Students, working in groups of about seven, chose
a play to produce. After many days of rehearsing, making cos-
tumes, props and sets, we wrote letters inviting families to come
and watch the performances. I wrote in my journal:

*On Wednesday afternoon the children performed their plays.
We had a very good turnout of family members. In between each play, students and parents wrote about what
stood out for them about the plays and performances. As I
watched the children and parents writing, I began thinking about how teaching language arts in a different way
this year has made it possible to invite families into the
classroom in meaningful ways. The basal wouldn't have
been able to provide these same opportunities. Beginning
the year with a wealth of fairy tales and folk tales from
many cultures provided a great opportunity for inviting
parents to read or tell their favorite tale to the class. It was
really natural how reading the tales spun in the book The*

People Could Fly led to families sharing and writing family stories and the class publishing a newsletter about them.

Now the class is writing I-search reports on famous African Americans. Jonathan has talked to me about exploring the life of a great-grandparent — someone he came to know through doing his family tree and story.

I eventually published Jonathan's paper — along with other writing about families — in the class newsletter:

This is a story about how my great-great-grandmother got from Africa to America. She was put on a ship. Her foot was tied to a ball and chain. She got off the ship and ran away. Before she died she was in Jacksonfiled.

Written by Jonathan Crawford and told to him by his Grandmother.

For our newsletter, Warren told the story of his mother:

My mother's name is Denise La Ruth Brown. She was born in 1958. She is now thirty-four years old. As a child my mother played rope, hopscotch, and played with doll babies. She was born in University of Penn. My mother's mother's name is Arlene Brown. She is fifty-nine years old. My mother's best food is chicken, oodles and noodles, and tea. Her favorite music is oldies music. My mother goes to church every Sunday. She sings in the youth ambassador choir. She is very strict sometimes and I do get upset with her but I know she's only doing it because she loves me. That's why I picked her to do my biography on!

by Warren

And Barry shared some interesting information about his grandmother:

> *Why My Grandmother Has Red Hair*
> *One day she went to the hairdresser and the lady commented*
> *you have a lot of gray in your hair. But you don't look old.*
> *She told the lady, "I don't feel old either," so they agreed let's*
> *do something about it. That is when she decided to dye her*
> *hair and chose the color red.*

Written by Barry

Future Directions for Inquiry

I spent two years looking closely and documenting events in my classroom connected to families and schools.

There were differences between the two years. In the first year, the Family Projects seemed to be central to making connections. During the second year, it was the phone conversations that were crucial to building and maintaining these relationships.

In trying to understand this difference, I returned to my journal and found the following entry from October 16, 1992:

> *It's been much more comfortable for me working with*
> *parents this year. In some ways, last year was most diffi-*
> *cult because I was so self-conscious about what I said to*
> *parents and how I said it. Unlike in past years when*
> *phoning parents was just something I did, this year it*
> *was my work that both colleagues and I would be look-*
> *ing at closely. This year I have more confidence in my*
> *instincts and have more knowledge gained from last year's*
> *looking. I feel more sure of what I'm trying to build be-*
> *tween families and schools.*

While there may be many more reasons for the differences,
it's significant to me that looking over time at my practice
with a community of colleagues can have such a positive
effect on my practice and, ultimately, the children.

Throughout both years, the books we read in the classroom
played a key role in the connections that were made between
home and school. These connections required a great deal of
time, something which is in short supply for teachers and parents. Mrs. Williams wrote that the only problem in doing the
Family Projects "was making time necessary to make the project
to be its best because of my working hours." Similarly, another
parent wrote, "My days are tied up with school. I can meet with
you during evening meetings." However, even with these time
constraints, many parents spoke favorably about the projects
they did with their children. In many cases these projects grew
out of conversations I held with these parents. I see these conversations as critical and necessary for developing the best educational program for their children.

Normally there had been two brief report card conferences sched-
uled for parents each year; the time was barely enough to give a
cursory summary of a student's work. As a result, I often felt
someone or something was being shortchanged.

My conversations with parents have allowed me to go beyond
these superficial encounters and have affected my attitude toward my job. At the end of the second year of my inquiry project,
I entered these thoughts in one of my final journal entries:

Now I have begun to think of many more ways to make
connections between the classroom and the family. Actu-
ally, it's not really a matter of just thinking of individual
activities but a matter of how I perceive teaching. Since I

believe that children learn from reading real books, all of my reading reflects that belief. If I approach children believing that a curriculum of connections between school and families makes sense, the units, lessons, and assignments are developed to encompass that belief, not just a writing assignment or a phone call home. What has been so exciting is how both of these beliefs, that of teaching through literature and making connections between families and school, support each other so beautifully.

Extending the Literate Community:

Literacy over a Life Span

by

DEBORAH JUMPP

S PRAWLED on a flat stretch of four city blocks in Philadelphia sits a majestic and venerable high school. The Gothic-inspired building has two massive towers, one over each of its main entrances. Granite steps with brick buttresses lead up to the entrances, which are flanked by cast bronze lanterns. On the sides of the building, carved stone grotesques recall a long-past era. Juxtaposed against this stately building, however, is a community imprisoned by poverty.

I am an African American high school English teacher who has spent 20 years working in schools such as this, grand old buildings where large numbers of students are now designated "at risk." These are schools

where many students have been identified as truants and delin-
quents, where teen pregnancy is high and where many students
have been retained for at least two years.

Within this building — as within the educational system at
large — the forces of tradition are colliding with the forces of
reform. As a teacher-researcher, I have been studying this conflict between custom and change specifically as it relates to standardized testing versus portfolio assessment. I have had serious
doubts about the traditional form of assessment which has students evaluated on a single piece of writing. By contrast, teachers in much of the country are employing portfolios as a more
authentic means of assessment.

About portfolios Courts and Amiran write:

> *Nowhere else can teachers see with such clarity the effects of
> their efforts in the classroom. It's all there, from awkward
> first draft to the clear demonstration of the growth of ana-
> lytical, evaluative and decision making skills evidenced by
> students' selection and reasoning in the introduction, the
> process of revision and the final drafts. Every portfolio dem-
> onstrates in concrete ways the growth in students' abilities
> to think reflexively and critically and to act on the results of
> such thinking* (Courts & Amiran, p. 107, in Belanoff &
> Dickson, 1991).

Despite such endorsements, few studies exist that examine
what happens when "disadvantaged" urban high school students
keep portfolios.

I decided to examine the use of portfolios among at risk students at two Philadelphia high schools. I focused on 43 students and five teachers (three English teachers — including

myself — a math teacher, and a social studies teacher, all of whom were team-teaching the same group of students.) The students were ages 15 to 17; the majority were African American, although Latino children were involved as well.

I set out to answer several questions ranging from "What counts as growth in writing?" to "How can portfolios help teachers make decisions about curriculum and instruction?" In this article, however, I wish to focus on a single question: "How can parents use portfolios?" To help answer this question, I solicited the cooperation of my students' parents. More than half — 26, in fact — agreed to participate in the project. Acknowledging the central role of parents, my goal was to use the portfolios as a way of building a literacy community that would extend beyond the school. Also, by inviting parents to take part in portfolio assessment, I would be increasing their involvement in their children's schooling.

What the Parents Saw
Students selected the writing they wanted to share with their parents from their writing folders. Their writing included journal entries, essays written about literature read in the classroom, writings about math projects and problem solving, and research papers that connected what was happening in the United States during particular time periods to what was happening in the local community during the same periods. The students typically selected one or two pieces for each assessment. Parents reviewed the selected pieces at home near the end of each marking period.

What I Asked Parents To Do with the Portfolios
To begin the project, I wrote a letter to the parents, explaining that I wanted to broaden the audience that my students' write for — so that they weren't just writing for the teacher — and asking them to become part of the audience for their child's

writing. I indicated that their involvement in the project would not require any special training, merely a willingness to spend some time with their child discussing his or her writing.

When the first pieces of student writing went home for parental assessment, I sent along a response form which asked the parents to focus on answering three questions about the writing their child had chosen to share:

- *What did you see in the writing?*
- *What did you like about the writing?*
- *What do I need to do as a teacher to facilitate your child's growth as a writer?*

These prompts gave parents an opportunity to be both advocates for their children and teachers, offering input into their children's education. In addition, as students began to discuss their writing with their parents, they not only strengthened their own literacy, but they began to hold conversations with parents about texts, working out meaning together; each parent and child was engaged in a significant literacy event.

I gave parents the option of responding to the portfolio pieces in writing or responding orally and having students write down their parent's response if parents were too busy to do this themselves. This strategy saved parents time and proved critical to maintaining their involvement in the project.

The Way Parents Responded to the Portfolios

The variety of ways parents responded to their children's writing helped me understand individual families and also gave me a better idea of what parents want for their children and expect of teachers and schools. I coded all the responses and categorized them in the following ways.

The most common response from parents voiced concerns about *grammatical competence:* word selection, punctuation, story structure or other matters related to form and correctness. The comments of Darryl's and Nikki's parents exemplify these types of responses:

"Darryl needs help with his grammar. He writes like he's talking to his friend on the corner."

"Nikki needs to put more details in the story and make it sound really interesting to catch the readers attention."

In conjunction with grammatical competence responses, many parents also made *correction responses.* In these instances, parents made actual corrections — mostly grammatical — to a student's work. Erica's mother changes the word "got" to the word "has" in the sentence in her daughter's composition that reads "He got a girlfriend." In fact, she goes through the entire composition, changing each use of the word "got" to the word "has." Joy's mother suggests she spell out words rather than use apostrophes, changing a sentence such as "They didn't have to walk far," to "They did not have to walk far."

With *encouraging responses,* parents commented that a student's writing was exceptional in some way or that the student showed potential as a writer. They also commented frequently on the knowledge their children had gained about the topics they'd written on. For example, Zora's mother comments during one assessment, "I liked the content of the essay. If someone knew nothing about Malcolm X, her essay would give them an informative, condensed version of his life." In another place she writes, "Zora is constantly telling me that she can't write, but after reading her essay I think that she can. She has problems with punctuation, spelling, grammar, capitalization, etc. If she can master the mechanics of writing, I think that she can become a good writer." Clearly Zora's mother is helping her daughter with her schoolwork, and the mother's assessment is similar to my own. I perceive Zora as a sophisticated writer who needs to mature more with the mechanics of writing.

Debbie's mother makes a similar comment. "With the right kind of help," she says, "Debbie can be an excellent writer. She writes every piece of my mail, envelopes, TV Guides and everything else." Debbie's mother reveals in her response some of the significant ways reading and writing are used in the home and the key role that Debbie plays in the literacy of her mother.

In making *informational responses*, parents specifically referred to the content of the writing. "This piece of writing tell me that my child has done a good job of research on Malcolm X," writes Kita's mother, "that now she may understand and have learned something on one of our Black leaders. What's liked about her writing is how she could tell of Malcolm's life history, from birth to death, in a short story form. She pointed out very good facts about his life."

In some cases, parents responded with *interpretive comments*. In one example, Lynnette's mother responds to Lynnette's writing by stating: "It tells me that she has piece of mind." To me, this statement was extrapolated from what the parent knew about Lynnette. Lynnette's peace of mind was not necessarily reflected in her writing.

At other times, parents responded with *personal comments*. In these cases, they made reference to issues or concerns that they had about their children; however, these issues were not mentioned in the child's writing. For example, Ernesto's mother notes, "He needs to be aware of how much help there is out in the world. There is always someone out to help you. Never try to get revenge … unless you're sure of the situation."

June's mother writes, "You have to be part of the solution not the problem. Be more open and think positive."

Debbie's mother writes, "Debbie wants to be fair, but everything is not always right or wrong."

In their *expectational responses*, parents consistently expressed concern that their children be proficient at writing standard English. They wrote that they expected me to encourage their children and to give them time and practice so that they could improve. Mrs. Chasse writes, "Zora needs to get over her fear of writing. She says she can't do it; therefore, in her mind, she can't. If Zora is constantly encouraged, than she might put more effort into her writing." Mrs. Addison, a grandmother involved in the project, writes, "If Derrick practice writing a little more, I think he will improve a great deal."

How Students and Parents Responded to Parent Assessment of Portfolios

The students enjoyed discussing their writing with the parents. On their response forms, which they filled out after each parent assessment and on which they indicated what the assessment had been like for them, they overwhelmingly reported that they were surprised that the parents were interested in their school work. Additionally, students were amazed that the parents were so encouraging to them as writers, which directly affected the view the students held of themselves as literate.

Latonya writes, "I think that my mother like the way that I think and the kind of imagination I have. She also likes the way I write."

Ernesto writes, "My mom surprised me by her getting into my school work. I should probably try to get her into more of my school work."

Tameka writes, "The thing that surprised me the most was when my mom told me face to face that the writing was well done and she think I should begin to do more writing."

Lastly, Keisha writes on her response form, "We both should do this more often even if she has to write and I respond to what she say." This response was particularly noteworthy because it shows Keisha transferring the peer conferencing format — in which students share writing with each other — to her home, transforming it into a technique she and her mother could put to use.

Parents' comments supported the notion that they want greater involvement with school and that the school may have to take the first step in establishing the relationship. When I had the opportunity to speak with parents during the school's Open House, many noted that this was the first opportunity they had had to interact in their child's schooling in this manner, indicating how pleased they were to be involved now.

Mrs. Coston stated, "I have never done anything like this before, not with any of my children, and I have had five children go through the school system."

LaQuita's mother said, "I had to meet the teacher that did this. I kind of liked this."

Warren's mother simply told me, "Thank you for allowing me to participate in Warren's education."

Conclusion

My work led to several findings. First, parents used these literacy events to create their own portfolio for their child. Specifically, their writing became a permanent record of their responses. They knew that by writing their responses (or having their responses recorded) rather than just talking, they were creating a document that their child could continually refer back to. Their comments were saved all year long.

Second, by taking part in portfolio assessment, parents became mediators in their children's learning. As mediators, the parents could intercede because they possessed knowledge about their children that I didn't have. For example, Zora never mentioned in class that she had a fear of writing. She participated somewhat reluctantly in peer conferencing, but I thought she simply had an introverted personality. Learning from her mother that she had a fear of writing allowed me to employ strategies to help ease her fear. If I had not provided parents the opportunity to respond to their children's writing, I would not have known about Zora's fear and been able to take steps to help her overcome it.

Finally, portfolio assessment empowered parents, giving them a way to make clear to me what they wanted for their children. Parents had been given a voice, and they used that voice to tell me what they felt their children needed from me to improve their writing. For example, Shawn's father writes, "This essay's composition and choice of grammar indicates that my child has to study English and read more." And Fatima's mother notes, "I do see as for my daughter to take more time and search her writing with more study and planning with all of her writing." In each case where I received a response like this, I wrote the parent a personal note to let them know how I would be following up on their suggestions.

Afterview

As a result of this project, students saw their writing as not just for the teacher, but for various audiences. Many of the students indicated that they never thought their parents could relate to their school work or that they would be able to have conversations about school work. Parents had a sense of really having a voice in their child's education and a confidence that a teacher would respond to their requests. The parents began to form a substantive partnership with the schools.

However, I think the person who grew the most from this research was me. I began to understand the potential of learning communities. I found that although I had started in one place, interacting with the students about their writing in the portfolio, I had moved beyond this dialogue as each student and I formed a triad with parents. As we began to construct knowledge together, we became a community of learners that respected one another. This community changed the dynamic between my students, their parents, and me.

I have continued to involve parents in writing assessment, not just in the classroom, but through professional development workshops to train other teachers in the process. Furthermore, as I have worked with community organizations I have been afforded the opportunity to talk to parents about portfolio assessment and continue to raise questions about the nature of ways teachers can involve parents in schools.

Educators and researchers need to address the implications of what parents want for their children and, at the same time, consider the ways we can help students achieve their goals. We cannot take a narrow view of literacy as simply the school practices of reading and writing. When we connect with families and build on their strengths and beliefs about literacy, we help educators and researchers see how to most effectively foster literacy. Lisa Delpit writes in *The Journal of Negro Education*:

> *Maintaining ignorance about community norms of parenting and child-rearing can lead to adversarial relationships with parents and the development among school people of a "messiah complex," that is the view that schools must save the children from their communities rather than work with communities toward excellence.* (Delpit, p. 238, 1992).

Literacy instruction should and can be thoughtful and respectful to both students and parents. Schools can and should be places where we expect learning to occur and where parents and teachers are partners helping to shape the future of students as literate adults.

All quotations from students and parents are presented unedited.

References
Belanoff, P., & Dickson, M. (Eds.). (1991). *Portfolios: Process and product.* Portsmouth, NH: Heinemann.

Delpit, L. (1992). Education in a multicultural society: Our future's greatest challenge. *The Journal of Negro Education, 61,* (3), 237-249.

"Are You the Teacher Who Gives Parents Homework?"

by

Carole Chin

EVERYONE knows what it means to be the parent of a fourth grader at this school:

It means the beginning of new things.

It means that there's a bus ride every day and you wonder whether your child will be safe.

It means it is both an exciting and scary time.

It means he [your child] has made the transition from a small school to a school twice the size of the primary school. He is reunited with old friends.

It means experiencing new things like doing homework at age 43.

With statements such as these, parents of my fourth graders responded to their first writing assignment. Along with a letter home welcoming them to the school, I had included a request that they try the same writing prompt I had used on the second day of class with their children. On that day, I asked students to write on the topic, "Everyone knows what it means to be a fourth grader," using as stylistic inspiration E. B. White's 1943 essay, "Everyone Knows What Democracy Is" ("It's the line that forms on the right. … It's an idea which hasn't been disproved yet. … Democracy is a letter to the editor. Democracy is the score at the beginning of the ninth. …") Now parents would write on the same topic, but with a twist: Everyone knows what it means to be the *parent* of a fourth grader.

And I know what it means to teach in my intermediate school — grades four through six — in the flatlands of a less affluent section of Berkeley, California. I know that most of the parents of the twenty-four children in my fourth grade class are anxious for their children to succeed and apprehensive about their well-being.

My fourth graders face a situation similar to kindergarten, since they are now the youngest children in the school. Their primary school had no more than 200 students; in this new school the student population is approximately 600.

Children are bused to school, a reflection of the District's policy of integration. Thus, my class reflects a racial mix with approximately 50% African American, 40% Caucasian, and 10% Hispanic and Asian students. Academically, the range goes from the first percentile to the ninety-ninth percentile on standardized tests. Children come from two-parent families, single-parent families, and families in which children are being raised by grandparents. Some families are affluent, others are on welfare. Four children are identified as ESL (English as a Second Language) students.

Everyone who will be attending the school has heard troubling rumors — daily fights on the school yard, green hot-dogs for lunch, intimidation by older students. For those students taking the bus for the first time, the realization that when something is amiss they can't walk home can be daunting to both parents and children.

It was in this setting that I decided I wanted to use writing to build a sense of community and to provide a forum for students and parents to express fears, anxieties, and concerns.

I wanted to keep track of what happened when parents and children wrote about the same subject. It was my belief that through writing a teacher can include those families who might otherwise feel alienated from the school; it's a way for parents to stay involved in their children's education. I was also interested in what effect, if any, the parental writing might have on the children. This was another form of communication for the children, the parents, and the teacher.

Parents responded enthusiastically to my homework assignment. I told my four ESL students to tell their parents to feel free to write in their native language which was either Mandarin, Cantonese, Japanese, or Korean. All of the parents in the class responded within five days. One parent wrote entirely in Chinese and one in Korean. I was concerned that I have an accurate translation of what the parents had written in their native language. One of the other parents had a doctorate in Chinese history and was fluent in both spoken and written Chinese. With regard to the response in Korean, I asked a professor at a nearby university if she could translate the parental response.

In translation, the Korean mother wrote about the experience her child had the year before and the hopes and desires she had for her child this year:

We came from Korea over one year ago. For both the children and the adults, life in the United States was very disorienting. After time passed, life settled down. We became more stable and got sensibilities back. Children can adapt to life in the United States much faster than adults.

The first school the children went to was a primary school. They adapted slowly. The children became interested in school. They made friends. More than anything else, they seemed interested in computers and science. After a year, they were very attached to the school. After my oldest child finished third grade, the child moved to the intermediate school.

She cried almost every night silently during that time. I asked why she cried. At first, she didn't say. But then the child said that she missed her friends and teachers. At that moment, my eyes watered. Even for her young heart, it must have been difficult for her to leave her first American school.

I cannot attend to my child's education. For that I am sorry and must apologize to the teachers and parents. But I am still hopeful and slowly getting through this difficult experience. I hope that my child will have the chance to learn to be independent.

Why did I want my parents to write? The last two sentences of this mother's "homework" precisely state my goal:

Only when skilled teachers and the parents of our children form a community will there be an education for the children. Then this will be a great school.

A response from the Chinese father, written in Chinese, was so moving that I felt that it was important to share his writing with all of the children and parents. Instead of responding to what it was like to be the parent of a fourth grader at the school, he wrote about the importance of writing:

> — *Writing is extremely important for one's whole life. If a person makes all kinds of mistakes in the ideograms and syntax in daily correspondences and messages, he will expose his own lack of literate skills and will not be respected. Besides, since this person cannot accurately express his own ideas, his whole life would run into roadblocks. He will not be able to find a good job; he will constantly make a fool of himself. On the other hand, if a person is very eloquent and can write well, he will be respected by society.*
>
> *Just take myself, for example. When I was in China, I was in the literary field. I was very skillful in Chinese. I could use the most beautiful, moving language to describe events, to compose poems, songs, and to create fiction. So I was recognized by society, respected by people. Just by writing I was able to support my family and led an upper-middle-class life. I could contribute to society. Ever since I came to the States, I couldn't even scribble a simple message. I couldn't find a good job. I can only function within the small confines of the Chinese community. Aside from enjoying the democratic freedoms of the United States, I have to start from the "ABC."*

I read parents' responses to the class as soon as they were brought in. They answered with sincere feeling and honesty. The responses from the non-English speaking parents gave all of us an insight as to what it is like to come to a new country where you need to learn a new language in order to communicate and to become part of the community.

I selected portions of each response and put them into two separate essays, one from the children and one from the parents. Later, I sent these papers home to the parents, introducing the children to the parents and to each other. Included in the student essay were responses such as:

> *It means you feel small even when you usually don't. It's not like being the oldest, it's being the youngest. Maybe the big kids will pick on you and tease you. When you're in fourth grade you feel like you're back in kindergarten.*

The parents essay included responses like:

> *It means the beginning of new things. It means the first time taking the bus. It means the school can be intimidating. As a parent I do worry about that big, rowdy playground.*

Even early in the school year, I was beginning to see the positive results of parents' "homework." Many parents, including English-speaking parents, are hesitant to come to school and enter the life of the school. However, these parents were eager to be part of the classroom community, and non-native speakers of English particularly welcomed the opportunity to write in their native language given this chance. One father made it a point to stop by the class on his way to work and tell me that he really enjoyed the writing and hoped that it would continue. The written parental response gave all the parents the opportunity to be part of the class. They didn't have to participate in "traditional" ways such as volunteering to tutor or be room mothers.

All of the parents came to our Back to School Night, held during the first month of school. In the past, non-English speaking parents have not participated in this event, and I believe that my initial request that they participate through writing made these parents feel welcome and very much part of this classroom community.

Because I was encouraged by parents' responses to the first request for writing, I wanted to continue to involve them in the writing, but I didn't want to impose. I had started a bulletin board called "Student of the Week" to give students an opportunity to become acquainted with each other. Students were responsible for the board, which included pictures and other artifacts that they wanted to share with the class. One of the students suggested that we ask the parents of the student of the week if they would either write, tape record, or come in and talk to the class and tell stories about that student.

A number of parents responded. Several wrote about their child, and others came in to talk to the class. The board created a safe writing environment and gave the parents an opportunity to teach. For example, in the midst of our sixth year of drought, one mother began her introductions of her son by writing:

> *The week before he was born, it rained so hard that our basement flooded! Nine years ago, it rained a lot.*

One of the first parents to write for the Student of the Week board said that this was the first time that her child had ever seen her writing something other than bills, that it had been a long time since she had written anything like this, and that she was quite nervous about how the class would react to her writing. She talked about how her daughter had spent days looking through the photo albums before making the final selection of about 12 pictures. The daughter then discussed in detail with her mother what she thought her mother should write:

Mitzi was born on a hot humid summer day in New York City. A delicious beautiful honeydew helped bring on the birth that day, so I often think of her as my honeydew. When Mitzi was a baby, she was easygoing, attentive, and a lot of fun.

Mitzi, her dad, and I moved from New York to the Bay Area when she was nine months old. She did not get a chance to pick up a Brooklyn accent. At ten months, she began swimming at Strawberry Canyon which has become one of our favorite watering holes.

Since she was two years old, Mitzi has enjoyed reading. She has also become an artist, making interesting projects, and beautiful ceramics and pictures. Mitzi has developed a strong, melodic singing voice which is often heard when she plays dress up. Mitzi attended a primary school from kindergarten to third grade and was in the Chinese Bilingual Program which taught her about Chinese culture and to speak some Chinese.

In her ninth year, Mitzi is a collector of Little Mermaid things, an avid reader of Sweet Valley Twins and the Boxcar Children, a fan of M. C. Hammer, and a good baker and cleaner-upper. She is very perceptive person, and we have lots of interesting talks. Mitzi cares very much about how the homeless and poor people are treated. I am very proud of her, and while I am writing about her my heart is smiling.

The board soon became more than just a place to meet each other. It was a reminder to the children that "our" parents do write, and it gave parents a way to work with children in a direct way, without conflict, since everyone wanted to accomplish the same goal — communicating information about the child and, sometimes, about the entire family. For example, Tami's dad wrote:

Best Friends

The day Tami was born at home on my bed, and started almost immediately sucking on my little finger, I knew she would be my best friend and sidekick for life. We do many things together but here are some of our favorite things to do:

1. "Check it out" — this is where I have to check out Tami's tickliest ticklish spots to make sure they are still working. When she laughs so hard she can't breathe, then I know they are working just fine.

2. "Flip out" — Tami will take a running jump into the air and in mid-air I will flip her over somersaulting onto the bed or couch.

3. "Shopping" — Tami and I do all the food shopping for our family. Her job, as I understand it, is to make me as crazy as possible by seeing how much she can make me buy that is not on our list. She is VERY GOOD at this game!

4. "Working" — Tami likes to help me whenever she can. At the shop she helps us answer the phones, and wraps presents for customers, and also helps Ron at the register. She even has her own time card!

I know some day Tami will outgrow some of these games, but I also know we will find other ways to play and be best friends, and I am looking forward to that. I am very blessed to have Tami as my daughter and best friend.

In addition to the writings from both of Tami's parents, her grandparents from Tennessee sent a card with a picture of themselves and Tami which included the following message to the class:

> *We are Tami's proud grandparents. We feel lucky to have*
> *such a loving and considerate granddaughter. She is loyal*
> *to family and friends and, we feel, pretty smart. The many*
> *things she undertakes she completes and enjoys. We hope*
> *she always continues to do good and caring things.*
> *— Gramma & Grampa*

When Tami's father finally came to the classroom, the students treated him like an old acquaintance.

One of the students, who had recently moved in with her grandparents, came to me and said that she didn't think she wanted to do the board. I told her to go home and ask her grandparents if they would help her. Her board included the following from her grandmother:

> *Latrice was born in Austin Texas in the early spring of*
> *1972. She was a beautiful baby and all the family was*
> *delighted because she was someone very special.*
>
> *Latrice's mom and dad moved to the Bay Area when she*
> *was three months old. She was a cheerful and active baby,*
> *fun to be with. When she was about three years old she*
> *loved to listen to music. She always fooled around with*
> *radios and other musical instruments. When she started*
> *talking, she always tried to sing and repeat words from*
> *songs. She loved music very much.*
>
> *Latrice has many tapes of songs and a collection of Barbie*
> *dolls, stuffed animals and books.*

*Latrice is a very friendly little girl and she has many friends
in the neighborhood where we live. We have faith in her,
and expect great things from her.*

All the children seemed to take interest in their parents' writings. In an interview, one parent said that she really had to think about what she thought the children would like to know about her son and what would not embarrass him. It turned out that all of the parental writing for the Student of the Week boards was edited by the children — or at least they made the attempt. Hannah's parents decided that they wanted to tell their unique, humorous version of how Hannah was born even though Hannah didn't want them to:

All three moons were out the night Hannah was born.

*It can be cold on Mars, but we were enjoying unusually
warm weather for the birthing season.*

*Over three million babies were born on that day our
Hannah was born. Parking was difficult that day and we
almost had to have her at school.*

*Hannah was born brilliant. She could play the piano and the
violin at the same time. She could also recite the King James
Bible from memory on her third day. By her fifth day she could
explain Einstein's misguided theory of relativity.*

*Since coming to the planet earth she has forgotten all of this
and believes a different story of her birth. But that is good
since we as a family are trying to fit in to the earth's society.*

*Hannah believes she was born on earth in the year of our
Lord 1982 on Friday March 5…*

All the parents, not only the English speakers and writers, contributed to their child's board. Mei's mother, a physicist who now works as a maid, wrote in Chinese which was then translated. Both the mother's writing and translation were part of the board:

> *My daughter, Mei, was born in Beijing, China, on Jan. 26, 1982. After a long and painful night, Mei was born at dawn, kicking and crying into the world. It happened to be Chinese New Year, so we can say that she was born on the dawn of a new year. This is why her father gave her the name Dawn. We also hoped that China would emerge from the darkness of totalitarianism into the dawn of modern democracy during her lifetime.*

Hiroshi's mother asked for an extra two weeks so that she could spend more time working on her story of Hiroshi. It was worth waiting for:

> *Hiroshi was born on December 13, 1981 in a small town in Japan, where the old inheritance system is still alive. Born to be a successor of a clan, he was celebrated like a prince, and was overwhelmed by gifts, courtesy and love. Both of his parents were not at all strict, and did not even try to be. Such a life during his infancy conditioned his present personality: Unambitious, but generous…*

The class was learning about each other through the parent writing. And we were also learning from these parents in a very special way about different cultures and traditions.

In addition to placing the parent writing on the bulletin board, parent writing was also featured in the weekly class newspaper. The parents, along with their children, looked forward to the Student of the Week feature. One mother said:

I've known some of these parents for years, and their writing shows a side of them that I've never seen before!

The approaching holidays suggested another piece of writing. I asked parents and children to discuss and write about a tradition, a holiday, or special occasion that the family observed or celebrated. Some parents wrote about their own childhood celebrations. Some parents planned the piece with the child. Some wrote their own paper on the same holiday that the child wrote about, while others wrote about a holiday of their own choice. In one family the child wrote a short paper about Thanksgiving, while his mother wrote a six-page paper about her family's celebration of Christmas in Pittsburgh. She described how exciting it had been for her to write about Christmas in her family:

It brought tears to my eyes. It made me realize how we've moved away from established family traditions since Dan and I started working. I was really moved by the experience. I feel that by my writing about Christmas it encouraged Jon to write more about Thanksgiving.

Many of my African American students and their families shared their experiences at family reunions:

Son: *Every year our family gets together in the Summer. The Summer before last Summer the family came here, then we went to L.A. We went to Disney Land for a day. Two days later we went to Mexico. We stayed there for three days and two nights. Just about all of the time we go to New York…*

Father: *Our family has always been very close. When we were small, my father always allowed other family members to live with us when they needed help. Uncles, aunts, cousins, and people who I had never seen before, stayed with us for short periods of time throughout my child-hood. Although the house was often crowded I learned to appreciate the sense of togetherness ... One of the things that has helped to keep us close is an annual family re-union. We don't have a set date or place for the reunion each year, but we never allow more than a year to go by before we get together. Sometimes a graduation brings us together. Last year it was my sister's wedding and the birth of my other sister's second child. What ever it takes, we find a reason to come together...*

A 1991 article in *Scholastic News* marking the fiftieth anni-versary of the bombing of Pearl Harbor pointed our student-family writing teams in a new direction. I wanted to call on family resources to help students learn more about World War II. Many children call December 7 "Pearl Harbor Day" but have absolutely no idea what it means or stands for. I realized that most if not all of the parents of the students were either too young or had not been born before or during the War.

The children went home and interviewed grandparents, aunts, uncles, and neighbors. For those students who were not able to locate anyone to interview, we found volunteer interviewees around the school. The class was learning about history from primary sources. One of the school secretaries, a second-gen-eration Japanese American woman whom the students knew as the one who answered their questions and soothed their wounds, responded to the questions as follows:

What do you remember best about the war?
My father was separated from us because he was taken by the F.B.I. but we were united in a camp.

What do you remember about the end of the war?
I was sad because my parents had to return to Japan and I had to stay in America.

Several children called their grandparents. Tami called her grandfather in Nashville and learned for the first time that her grandfather's brother had been killed in the war. Hiroshi's grandfather in Japan answered:

What do you remember best about the war?
I was safe from the atomic bomb.

What do you remember about the end of the war?
Good because I didn't have to go to war. The war ended two days before I went to the front battle. I was not strong enough for a soldier, so I did not have to go to fight unlike young people of my age.

I stayed in several cities in Japan preparing for battle. I spent most of my time in Hiroshima. On August 4, I was ordered to join the front battle and I move to Shikoku.

It was just two days after I moved to Shikoku that the atomic bomb was thrown to Hiroshima on August 6 in the morning.

The order to move to Shikoku saved my life accidentally.

We had just finished reading *Sadako and the Thousand Cranes*, about the bombing of Hiroshima. When I finished reading the Japanese grandfather's interview, the children looked at Hiroshi in wonder. Finally, one of the children said, "It's a good thing he left Hiroshima on August 6, otherwise you wouldn't be here today." Hiroshima and the atom bomb became a reality for the children through this interview.

The children were so intrigued with the World War II interviews that I asked the parents to share their memories of another historic event, the death of Dr. Martin Luther King, Jr.
Many of the parents had stark memories of that event. Gregory's
godmother was visiting the night of this assignment and she
shared her memories with us:

> I was attending John Adams Junior High School in Los Ange-
> les, California. Like many of my classmates, I thought it was
> going to be just another school day. It started out that way, just
> another school day that is, until the announcement came over
> the loud speaker … Dr. Martin Luther King had been shot
> and killed on a balcony in Alabama. The silence was so heavy
> in the classroom, and the school, that it held everyone in their
> places, as if frozen in time. After moments, tears began to fall.
> The teachers, people who you thought didn't have emotions,
> were just crying. No one could think, everyone just reacted. I
> remember the death of Dr. Martin Luther King as a point in
> history and time when the entire nation felt a great loss simul-
> taneously and wept!

> School was closed early and I walked home in silence. Once
> home, my family was glued to the television and radio, not
> wanting to miss any bits of information and yet hoping in
> my young mind that there had been a mistake, that the
> announcement was some kind of sick joke. Every time I
> saw his face, heard someone mention his name or heard his
> voice, a solemn feeling would cover my body.

> Till this day, many years later, the sound of his voice or the
> mention of his name causes me to stop in my tracks, frozen
> and remember. The feeling of loss is something I will have
> to live with for the rest of my life. For I shall never forget
> Dr. Martin Luther King, Jr.

One mother shared her vivid childhood memories:

I was living in Mississippi at the time of his death. I was only 8 years old, but I remember. I remember sitting in the living room looking at TV when the newsman came on saying that Dr. Martin Luther King Jr. had been killed by a white man whose name was James Earl Ray who hated him and all blacks. I was very sad, tears running down my face as I looked at my mother all in tears. She was so sad, mad, upset to hear the bad news about Dr. Martin Luther King Jr.

I asked my mother why did they kill him and who are they? I wanted to know. Then I saw on TV that the white people really hated blacks. I had the feeling even at the age of 8 years old. I was thinking about what is going to happen to us now? Will they kill us now? I was full of fear. I thought the white man was going to kill me because my skin was black. I would not go to sleep, the fear of the white people wouldn't leave me alone. For days I stayed in the house with my mother, seeing more tears roll down her face day in day out. My thoughts were that the white man that killed Dr. King is going to hell for killing our leader that black leader of the black people. He killed the body but not the soul.

My feelings were pain so much pain. Sadness to know that Dr. Martin Luther King Jr. had been killed by bad white people who hated black people that wanted to have peace and freedom. Hoping we shall overcome one day.

When I interviewed this mother, she said:

This assignment helped me to improve my writing. It gave me the courage to try the GED for the third time and I passed!

I typed up the Martin Luther King essay and I entered it into a contest and I was the grand prize winner. You not only helped my son you helped me. I thought well, she asked the parents to do this and this is my practice essay here. Shoot, it gave me the courage to write an essay. When you asked me to do that my mind went all the way back. I remember the names. I'm good. It inspired me so much. I thought if she can give these 4th graders this assignment, I'm 32 and I can do it too!

I stayed up until 3 o'clock in the morning. I said to myself this is what I am going to write about.

I cried ... all this is happening again. My mother working for the white folks. It hurted me all these memories. I will never forget.

I want to be a writer. I said, "God give me the strength. You can give me the third eye."

At first I put it aside but said, "No I am going to this for my child. My mom couldn't read or write but I can. So, I'm going to do it for both my mom and my son."

My son has a book on Martin Luther King that he takes to bed every night. I asked him to let me look at it. He said, "No, you have to think about it." My boyfriend took the book home that night. I started to write. I wrote a paragraph and then I cried. I wrote another paragraph and cried.

I brought back all those memories. My mom was helping hold us together while working for those white folks. They called us "Nigger." Nigger isn't a certain person.

I couldn't have done it if you hadn't inspired me. I wrote it to my son and he and I talked about it. He asked me to read it to him. He asked, "Did that really happen?"

I said, "Yes. Here today black and white kids play together. Blacks and whites get married. But not back then in Mississippi. It's part of our history."

I read it to my class. I had tears as I read and people cried. It made my best friend remember things that had happened to her. At the end of the reading I trembled and said, "Why?" I felt like this man gave us something to grow on. He set us free. It's still happening, but we cannot let them tell us.

Ms. Chin you are the reason I won this award. I never thought I could do this. You don't know it but you are my teacher.

The Contributors

HOWARD BANFORD teaches second and third grade at the Glen Cove Year-Round School in Vallejo, California. Increasingly over the 13 years he has been teaching, he has worked to "get deep" into his students' thinking, seeking them out to help him understand what is working in his class and what isn't. "When I'm confused, I turn to the students," he says. These days, he spends many of his out-of-class hours introducing his one-year-old daughter to the pleasures of Bay Area cafes. Together they continue the search for The Great Cappuccino.

MYRON BERKMAN has moved from his job at Newcomer High, where he taught for 13 years, and now teaches E.S.L. at Mission High in San Francisco. Before Myron became a teacher, he served with the Peace Corps in Cambodia. He is the author of *Our Lives*, a book for E.S.L. students published by Linore Publishing. Myron says of his teaching: "Even though teaching gets harder all the time, sometimes when I close my classroom door, the magic happens. That's enough to keep me going."

CAROLE CHIN now teaches fourth grade at Le Conte School in Berkeley, California. Until this year, Carol taught at Malcolm X Elementary School, also in Berkeley, the school that is the setting for "Are You The Teacher Who Gives The Homework?" Carol herself went to fourth grade in Berkeley, but in those days, as she tells her students, everyone walked to school: "No one had the chance to take the school bus." Carol and her husband train Labrador retrievers, a hobby in which they will soon be including their four-year-old daughter, Mara.

CHRISTINE CZIKO taught in New York City junior and senior high schools for 23 years. In 1993 she became part of the founding faculty of a "New Visions" high school in Manhattan, the School for the Physical City. She is currently teaching English at Thurgood Marshall Academic High School, a new public school in the southeast corner of San Francisco.

BOB FECHO, now in his 21st year as a teacher in the School District of Philadelphia, teaches English at Simon Gratz High School. Bob is a co-founder — along with his colleagues Natalie Hiller and Marsha Pincus — of Crossroads, an inquiry-based school within a school now in its sixth year. When he isn't teaching, Bob plays guitar, frequents films and brandishes bad puns.

DEBORAH JUMPP has for 20 years been a teacher of middle school and high school English in the School District of Philadelphia. Presently, Deborah is a teacher on special assignment to the Philadelphia Education Fund. Previously, she was the Writing Coordinator of the Research Apprenticeship Program, providing theoretical and practical expertise for improving the teaching of writing and literacy skills. She has made numerous presentations at national conferences, including The National Reading Conference and The National Conference of Teachers of English. She has co-authored a teacher's manual for the *Philadelphia Inquirer* entitled *Using the Newspaper with the Pennsylvania Comprehensive Reading Plan.*

CAROLE MILLER teaches a class of bilingual second graders at the Charles Sumner School in Boston. She has been a classroom teacher for 24 years. Among her prize possessions is a student drawing of himself atop a large rock formation that the class had climbed on a field trip, his arms outstretched above his head in victory. The drawing symbolizes for Carole the increased confidence and self esteem which come with taking risks, something she encourages in her classroom. Carole enjoys "civilized" English murder mysteries, afternoon tea, cozy inns and exploring the coast of Maine with her husband.

Marci Resnick currently teaches second grade at the Emlen Elementary School in The Philadelphia School District. With 20 years of teaching experience, Marci has been an active teacher consultant with the Philadelphia Writing Project since 1990. Outside of class, Marie enjoys being with her husband and two children.